YO-BYO-038

CONCILIUM

Religion in the Seventies

CONCILIUM

Concilium, May 1977: Fundamental Theology

CHRISTIANITY
AND SOCIALISM

Edited by

Johann-Baptist Metz and
Jean-Pierre Jossua

A Crossroad Book
The Seabury Press · New York

1977
The Seabury Press
815 Second Avenue
New York, N.Y. 10017

Library of Congress Catalog Card Number: 77-90100
ISBN: 0-8164-03635-1
ISBN: o-8164-2148-x (pbk.)
Printed in the United States of America

CONTENTS

Editorial

CHRISTIANITY and socialism is a theme that can be stated and assessed appropriately only in a universal perspective. Hence it has been chosen as a specific topic for this journal, which is concerned with international and intercontinental communication in the Church and in theology.

The question of the connection of Christianity with late capitalism and socialism is no longer soluble merely in terms of the so-called east-west antithesis. For the north-south antithesis is increasingly overlaying that older prospect. By this latter opposition, we mean of course the dichotomy between the rich industrial countries of the North and the poor southern regions whose population is for the most part traditionally Catholic. This north-south antithesis cuts through the universal Church, and takes effect, for example, in the relation of the mid-European and North American Church to that of the Latin American sub-continent. The question of the relation of Christianity to late capitalism and socialism is therefore an eminently ecclesiastical theme. That does not mean that we can make the usual ecclesiological reduction. Instead it enables us to see the topic in an appropriately Christian perspective. It is not a theme to be treated quite neutrally, as might happen when individual countries are classified from without according to their various social systems, so that the situation of Christians and the Church within those systems is assessed exactly in that way.

The topic of this issue is much more an urgent question addressed to the Church itself. Just as the Gospel announced by the Church must always be a challenge to social and political life, so the north-south antithesis we have mentioned must become a thorn in the Church's side but also an inspiration to it. What is the Church to do about the obvious class distinctions between North and South when both regions are in fact within the Church? How can they be reconciled with the living unity of the Church? How are they to be reconciled with the Church as the one eucharistic community, the sign of eschatological oneness? What is the Church to do about the fact that within it many individuals, indeed entire nations, live in such degraded circumstances that they can hardly be called human? Can the rich churches of the North salve their consciences towards the poor churches of the South be means of a form of almsgiving that has been shown to be an apparatus of exploitation and structural injustice?

The topic of Christianity and socialism is examined here in an issue usually devoted to questions of 'fundamental theology'. This serves to express our conviction that whenever theology is fundamentally concerned with its proper ends, it is always politically engaged; that accords with the notion of practical fundamental theology as political theology. It insists on the mystico-political constitution and dual commitment of faith. This kind of fundamental theology does not make the Kingdom of God the goal of politics and economy. But it insists that the Kingdom of God should not be indifferent to the cost of world markets. It does not confuse God with a utopia to which no one prays. But it insists that religion can earn no greater guilt than from showing its political innocence through non-participation. If the Christian religion is political because it proclaims the dignity of the individual, of the subjective existence of all men and women before God, then it has to stand up for that individuality where it is most endangered. It must not only fight to ensure that people remain individuals, but so that they can grow out of their situation of poverty and oppression to become individuals. That is part of the cost of orthodoxy.

This issue is essentially concerned to offer information and documentation. It serves to orientate readers puzzled by a complex of problems too often discussed within the Church only in apologetical and polemical clichés. It is divided according to the simple pattern of conventional political geography: western capitalist countries (articles from Arbeloa/Robles to Füssel)—socialist countries (cf. Hücking, Stehle, Fetscher)—the Third World (the contributions of Quoc-Hung to Ellacuria). There is some progression from informative articles to more systematic contributions.

We have had to restrict ourselves and therefore we could only treat the theme selectively and paradigmatically. There is no point in listing all the topics that are missing. The theme will certainly return, even more urgently.

J. B. METZ
J. P. JOSSUA

Giuseppe Ruggieri

Christianity and Socialism in Italy: Semantic and Theological Reflections

THE Church in Italy can tell of repeated and differing approaches to conciliation between Christian faith and socialism over the last hundred years. It is hard to see how these efforts could have achieved success, even though they all represent aspects of the same movement.

The aim of this article is not one of historical reconstruction. It will focus on a specific aspect of the phenomenon, that of the words actually used. Any meeting or process of assimilation produces its own climate. The elements which make it up each time have a claim to make new sense, that is, one apart from the one they had in their original context. Often that claim cannot be substantiated. The elements which came from the different contexts fail to give fresh meaning in the new climate because of the resistance put up by the previous context, which is jealous of what it gave birth to having a life of its own, away from its originator. This jealousy is felt by both the Church and the socialist movement and it has been behind the failure of most of the various attempts to synthesise Christianity and socialism in Italy. An account of it shows that it has developed like the abandoning of the parents by the child.

In order to illustrate this point I would like to refer to three especially significant episodes in the story of the *rapprochement* of Christians and socialists in Italy. Two of them come from the past while the other is contemporary. In chronological order they are religious popular socialism from 1880 to about 1920, the 'Catholic Communist' movement and the drive towards socialism by Christians.

RELIGIOUS POPULAR SOCIALISM

With the possible exception of the modernistic 'socialist Christians' who were grouped round the periodical *Nova et Vetera,* and the influence Swiss and French religious socialism had on isolated Italian Protestants, Italian religious socialism was popular. It was in no way a Christian movement so much as a general awareness that the socialist movement wanted to bring about in the Catholic masses between 1880 and, roughly, 1920. Because of its very nature it is easy to spot the beginnings of this popular 'education' in innumerable socialist pamphlets and magazines of the period, and it is correspondingly difficult to judge its range. At all events, it was an educative effort which put down very deep roots; it goes a long way to account for the fact that the mass of Italian Catholics find it easy to reconcile traditional religion with belonging to Marxist groups. In *Quaderni del carcere* (Prison Notebooks) Antonio Gramsci describes the nature of the 'reformation' this educative process had in the masses:'. . . the intellectual and moral (that is to say, religious) "reformation" of the people in modern times happened in two phases . . . the second time came with the spread of ideas central to, and often taken from, the philosophy of praxis, tinged by the philosophy of illuminism, and subsequently by scientific theories of evolution. The fact that such a "reformation" was disseminated crudely and by means of little pamphlets does not diminish its importance in history; it would be hard to credit that the mass of the people influenced by Calvinism could take in ideas of a more elaborate and refined nature than those in the little pamphlets. . . .'[1]

The attitude expressed by this socialist propaganist in the book creates a difficulty for the Christian. For one thing, it justifies anticlericalism and explains what lies behind it; it is the Church that has declared war on socialism. 'Instead of attending to religious matters and their proper function, priests began to meddle in politics so as to support the employers and to denigrate and fight socialists.'[2] In other words, the antagonism towards the Church shown by socialists derives from the opposition that the Church puts up against socialism. By refusing to mediate with the Church, socialists want to discredit the profound appeal of Christianity. Christianity is thus 'the need felt by the poor for redemption';[3] moreover, socialism invests Christ's word with a new meaning.[4] The differences between socialism and Christianity do not lie in the nature of the aim, which is one and the same, but in the ways of achieving that aim. Christianity makes efforts to reach that goal by preaching Christian love; socialism recommends 'justice because [it] sees that charity is unfortunately not enough to dry the tears of the disinherited'.[5] The result of this concession made by Christianity is the growth of the image of a 'Socialist Jesus' who comes somewhere between kitsch and an illuminist vision.[6] Jesus is the initiator of a movement to free the oppressed. This all began long ago. Socialists revere the great martyr of the past, Christ. Some members of the socialist party circulated a picture of Jesus raising Lazarus from the dead; Christ looks like Karl Marx and Lazarus looks like a worker.

By using such propaganda methods, socialism is able to appear as a 'faith' in human values, such as freedom and justice. One often hears the phrase 'socialist faith'. Such a faith is thought capable of ridding the people of the useless manifestations of traditional deviation in their religious feeling.[7] Unlike what follows later, socialism is not seen as 'historical materialism' or a split in a materialistic account of history.[8] No, it is a 'socialist' vision of the world which receives a religious interpretation.

Whenever this vision is welcomed by Catholics it is made out to be 'supernatural'. Socialist maxims reinforce those of the Old and New Testaments; thus socialism is sanctioned, holy, seen to be acting out the will of God, and when it is written or spoken about, socialism is seen as being inspired and driven forward by someone 'up there'.[9]

CATHOLIC COMMUNISTS

Catholic Communists represent a complex movement which has had a short but productive history. They have a large following, mostly in Rome and Central and Northern Italy. They can lay claim to having a new, possibly even a unique, approach in the confrontation with Marxism. The movement derived from various groups of Catholics who were living in Rome towards the end of the fascist régime and who felt deeply critical towards it. The actual name 'Catholic Communists' appears, after a number of other titles, on 18 September 1943. Then, at a meeting in the Visconti Lyceum in Rome (13 September 1944), the movement became the Party of the Christian Left (P.S.C.) The congress, which was held from 7 to 10 September 1945, saw the disbanding of the party and the end of the experiment. It is not going too far to say, however, that those who lived through that experience were also those who did more to bring Catholics and Communists face to face, and that in a far more decisive and far-reaching way, than anyone else has done.[10]

What is new about Catholic Communists? In the first place they took up the differnce between historical materialism, which is acceptable to Christians, and the philosophic vision of dialectical materialism in a completely original way. The distinction which had already been accepted by socialist Modernists, was taken up again from two special points of view. In the first instance it was linked to an effective practical policy and was not confined to intellectual discussion nor was it simply a shift of opinion. 'To be a Catholic Communist simply means accepting political ideology and the practical politics of Communism as the best possible means of resolving the present very painful contradictions in modern society. It also means not accepting from these same instruments the purely metaphysical aspects which exclude us from practical politics and the rise and development of Marxism'.[11] Thus we recall that Communism is an ideal and a heritage independent of Marxism to which Marxism brings the benefit of a scientific instrument. In the second place the originality of Catholic Communists, and one which they feel distinguishes them from most of the others who have attempted to reconcile Christianity and socialism, comes in their unconditional commitment to the Catholic Church, including the magisterium, in the daily practice of their faith. They feel very much part of the Church for all that they repudiate the doctrine of the Church on social matters since its 'political' force is in decline. They especially disagree with the use of a tactical obedience which draws a distinction between the infallible and the fallible. The Catholic Church is the result of the will of Christ that man should be saved. It is therefore invested with a dimension above and beyond history. 'It is only the Catholic Church, despite all compromises, its mistakes, its petty regulations over political and temporal matters, which carries on the teaching of traditional dogma in a pure and uncorrupt state. It is in it, now as ever, that we can find exactly the spiritual premiss for our revolutionary work, despite the fact the Catholic politics may seem rather reactionary. Christian dogma is not history; it is above and beyond history; revelation was not made by man, but he receives it. The progressive man who turns from civilization cannot alter it; he has, however, to make it valid in history somehow or other . . . that very theological idea is not a static phenomenon, the simple repetition of revealed dogma; it is a perennial attempt to adjust to it by means of human words, which are, in the nature of the case, historical. . . .'[12]

These quotations were selected so as to illustrate the non-conforming attitudes felt by Christian socialists at the present moment and are representative of a great many others.

The distinction between historical materialism and dialectical materialism did not have the effect of making Catholic Communists regard the relationship between science and ideology as a simple one. Every science is inevitably linked to a philosophic vision. Indeed as a result of this essential connection and because of the fundamental philosophic need for a scientific version of reality, historical materialism has looked for the support of a philosophy which would satisfy 'the two fundamental requirements of the discovery: the existence of matter and a forward-looking interpretation of history'. The essential advance made by historical materialism is in recognizing 'that the political struggle is not the opposite of autonomous religious or philosophic concepts which later translate themselves into political reality; on the contrary, it is the struggle of material economic interests in search of ideologies and myths with which to defend themselves'; when historical materialism developed 'none of the existing philosophic theories at the time were able to fulfil both requirements . . . with one exception—the materialism of Feuerbach'.[13]

This link between philosophy and historical materialism which was necessary historically speaking is, nonetheless, capable of change. Indeed it is possible that historical materialism might have been able to find a greater degree of justification than that offered by dialectical materialism. Christianity offers this way out if it is felt with moral passion from within the progress of events and history. A 'moral passion' which unmasks unholy alliances, wrong conditioning by religion, is, just because of that, 'the way in which the Christian spirit infiltrates Marxism. Moreover, this theory provides the true justification, as dialectical materialism in its published formulaion does not, of its own need which, despite its metaphysical dogma, resides, obscurely but irrefutably, in the huge and memorable figure of Marx'.[14]

Indications of a hard-core attitude[15] to be seen in these positions were put right by the on-going history of Catholic Communists and by events themselves. The P.S.C. based itself on the hypothesis of most Catholic parties[16], but its 'self-immolation' implied that it had definitively overcome the misunderstandings implicit in that position. The label 'Catholic' or 'Christian' is fundamentally opposed to what Catholic Communists went on repeating, which is that the party is the outcome of history and therefore of class and that a single united party of Catholics would be ideologically unsound since it implies a mystification of the material basis of the political struggle.[17] Therefore the 'self-immolation' of the movement may well prove to have been its most important act and, because its participants know how to carry it on into the future, its most seminal as well.

CHRISTIANS FOR SOCIALISM

It is difficult to evaluate this movement which came out of Chile in 1971. It was formed in September 1973 as far as Italy is concerned and it has shown that it can fill a gap for a multiplicity of groups: communities founded on a Christian basis, critical Christian periodicals,

Christian-inspired union policies, groups of the A.C.L.I. (Catholic trade unions), etc. This mixture of views puts one on the alert since quite different points of view on matters of supreme importance co-exist in the movement. The only two documents which ought to be considered 'official' are the winding-up proceedings of the Congress of Bologna (21–23 Sept. 1973) and the congress held in Naples (1–4 Nov. 1974). I will present material from these two documents which are to the point in this discussion.[18]

Christians for Socialism (CPS) do not want to become a party organization. They like to be thought of as 'a point of reference not only for the vanguard but also for the mass of Christian people who are in the process of freeing themselves from clerical corporatism and from the class aims of demochristianity' (CNT, 10 Nov. 1974, p. 8). The CPS do not want a confrontation of Marxist ideology with Christian ideology so much as to 'evaluate what it means for comrades who have faith and who agree with the scientific analysis and the revolutionary project of the working class, as Marx's theses are put into practice.' For them, it is not a case of search for a 'Christian specific' which would distinguish between the political act of a Christian and that of a non-Christian, but a desire to understand what political experience with the working class has on one's faith. This puts them, as far as the Church goes, in a conflict which some of them describe as 'rupture yet faith'.[19] The Church's position is a difficult one, not least because both Catholics and Protestants are members of CPS. The Catholics tend to emphasise the connection between faith and politics while Protestant Christians tend to dwell on the importance of transcendent faith.

'Socialism' as far as the CPS is concerned, can be expressed by the following vague sentence: 'to say socialism is not enough . . . we have not got a perfect model to impose on reality, nor have we got a reality that is without problems, but we do have a combination of forces and historical experience which requires varification and precise choices . . . This verification and those choices . . . must be put into practice by militant methods and by means of the various organizations which are already in existence.' (Com, 30 Sept. 1973, p. 4).

They refer frequently to the difference between historical materialism and dialectical materialism to be found in Marxism and sometimes even claim to have overcome them (F. Gentilone in Com, 9 Dec. 1973, p. 3, in which he sums up positions held by various writers). It looks as though by declaring themselves to have resolved the difference between historical materialism and dialectical materialism, some members of the CPS want to say that the confrontation between faith and Marxism should be seen as global, while remaining a matter of discussion, and that it is not appropriate to take one element out of a single historical event. Naturally the class war is seen as an up-to-date version of Christian love. Indeed it is the new theological position (Gentiloni in Com 9 Dec. 1973, p. 3). This idea echoes an element in the religious popular socialism of yesteryear; for charity to mean something it must be expressed in the actual struggle of the oppressed. Socialism is the only possible position from which to build more just and free relationships between men. Thus it becomes not only legitimate, but it makes perfect sense for the faithful Christian to choose socialism. The choice of socialism 'has become the only practical reality which makes sense when we ask ourselves the real meaning of our faith, and it provides the witness which we, as believers, are called upon to make' (CNT, 17 Nov. 1974). These, then, are the two positions most frequently to be seen in the CPS: a materialist interpretation of the Bible and class analysis applied to the Church.[21] Belo leads the way in a materialist reading of the Bible, the primary function of which is to highlight Christ the 'subversive' (CNT, 13 Nov. 1975, p. 5). Not all CPS members are happy with this tendency. For some of them it only means that one cannot read the Bible in a neutral way. It does not follow that Marxism carries with it a correct reading of the Bible. On the other hand, it is true that a reading of the Bible cannot take into account the political and historical stage of the person reading it and that 'Christ's coming makes sense to the working class, as well as to Marxists . . . and that this is the way we interpret 'transcendent nature and the ''infallibility'' of the Church' (CNT, 30 Nov. 1975, p. 11).

Thus a materialist analysis of the Church does not seek to name it as a class enemy but it indicates that ecclesiastical institutions 'have too often acted . . . in obedience to cultural pressures and power blocks which have little to do with evangelism and a great deal to do with the ruling classes' (F. Passuello in CNT, 3 Aug. 1975, p. 6).

The uneasiness shown by the ecclesiastical institution is taken by the CPS to mean a more or less complete refusal to make room within the established Church for a position taken as a result of the practical application of faith. This refusal matches the privelege afforded to communities founded on Christian principles. They are seen as 'primary and essential tokens of the sacrament' in the Church today, and are thought of as necessary in an attempt to live and to apply one's faith, 'for it is in the present, not in the past or the future, that a Christian lives out his fundamental relationship to the coming of Jesus Christ' (F. Gentiloni in CNT, 13 Apr. 1975, p. 6).

This look into these communities, which are fundamentally Christian and which guarantee a real application of faith, gives rise to fears that they will invalidate other attempts to find faith (cf. G. Franzoni in CNT, 17 Nov. 1974, p. 8). Therefore it is not only from the Church's point of view but also from that of the mass of the poor that there sometimes creeps in a doubt as to whether or not the CPS constitutes 'one of the responses given by the bourgeoisie and the young bourgeois in particular whose aim is, and this with the maximum degree of virulence, to dismantle the capitalist system' (G. Lutte in CNT, 1 Dec. 1974, p. 8).

CONCLUSION

Let us first of all look at the wavering meanings the word 'socialism' (or even 'communism') has acquired: It sometimes means 'religiously', carrying the idea of justice; in another context it is 'the means of political struggle'; and at other times it is taken to signify the convergence of ideology and struggle. Sometimes the word is taken as being the equivalent of Marxism, sometimes it is not. One can see therefore that it is not the use of the word itself which is a problem to Christians. This semantic vagueness is indicative of a perennial desire expressing itself in these various different ways. And what is that desire?

All three of these interpretations, which I have so briefly analyzed, reveal the steady figure of the 'Church': denied, accepted and apologetically 'dragged' towards a working class which is understood, of course, to be a long way off and which is identified with the communities. It seems to be the case that the desire is one for the modern Church to make common ground for Christ and man, beginning with frustrated working man. The unique history of the various attempts to reconcile Christianity and socialism is therefore a story of the desire for the Church to mediate. It is no accident that the theme of belonging has always been at the forefront, especially as they have thought of themselves as having overcome the very problem of Church membership.

If the varying meanings of 'socialism' betray a desire for the Church to mediate, and the various encounters between Christianity and socialism are the result of a response to faith, that is, they are a practical apologia. And, just as with any apologia, it is the new direction taken each time which restructures what might otherwise be a quiet discussion of faith. This path taken does not lead away from Christianity for it is Christians themselves who are indissolubly linked to the history of man. If that history is one of socialism and the class struggle they themselves ought to be aware of the hope that lodges in their breasts and they ought to discover their faith within the new events in history which determine it.

The Church's attitude towards these new experiences is an uncomfortable one: it is the result of changes brought about in its own position because of the introduction of elements which have not yet been absorbed into the Church. However it is impossible to absorb them without upsetting the traditional equilibrium of their position and without their being upset in turn. Two factors in particular dominate possible changes in that position at the present time; they are ideology and scientific knowledge.

Historically speaking, socialism sets its face against religion and Christianity in particular. This is true of Europe, at any rate. But it was not always the case. One can clearly trace the origins of socialism and Communism to a religious source. It is in order to answer a religious need that Communism seeks to rationalize its conviction that it is only in radical communion with the divine in himself and others like him that man arrives at the truth and fulfils his destiny. It is not by chance that the first formal expression of Communism in the modern world is to be found in the works of Thomas More. It was written during the first stage of capitalist accumulation in England in the sixteenth century when country gentlemen appropriated land for their private use from what had been traditionally held common land by means of 'enclosures'. A religious conscience was aroused to deny a power which allots goods to certain people exclusively. On the other hand, social science in the nineteenth century joined forces with Communist ideology, broke off with religion and, in an epic turnaround, put itself in the position of an atheist. This version of atheism was determined by dialectical materialism and was the means whereby a set of values proved capable of stirring up and justifying the actions of whole generations. This shows that the 'conversion' of the ideologically based socialist cannot be achieved by means of a simple distinction between historical materialism and dialectical materialism. 'Historically' speaking the ideology of dialectical materialism is not without a purely negative function and it could easily be discarded as a useless and damaging excrescence. Socialism in history shows itself to be coherent in meaning and direction.

It is not only the use of a Marxist scientific interpretation of history within a differing hermetic position (although it is also that!) but more the apologia applied to a *different* aspect of history with all that it entails (including ideology). This apologia has not yet been devised; theology is a body of knowledge which follows after the exercise of faith in its historically determined position; it cannot anticipate it with a theory. Theology ought, perhaps, to concern itself with the following two propositions.

The first of them is that the entire world-wide Church, and not only a small part of it (and most certainly not the 'purist' element shown in recurrent Montanism), is the proper argument to present. The second proposition concerns a corrective to the continual application of 'socialism' in connection with the application of 'charity' and the workings of 'justice', from which it follows that the class struggle is a practical version of that sense of justice. This claim to merge charity with justice forces a Christian to ask himself if it does not include a denial of Jesus Christ and his irreducible nature. In the face of the failure of the law (no less serious than the failure of charity in history) it is perhaps important to stress that the salvation of man does not lie in an easy amalgam (in the confusion between the law and the teachings of the Gospel, between the Old and the New Testaments, between knowledge and aspiration, between necessity and freedom), but in a respectful and questioning support of everything which goes to make up civilization.

This historic tradition, clearly expressed, recognizes three categories which Pascal classified as being those of the body (appetite, knowledge and necessity), of the spirit (freedom, thought and desire) and of charity (grace, love and Jesus Christ).[23]

It would be easy to see these three categories either as a dialectic triumph in which case each category takes care of the one preceding it, or as a unity in itself by means of which man may realise himself in one or other of the three. The historical divisions which man lives through, not only in his personal life but in the burning division of universal history, call for them to be reunited but not by means of reduction or by absorbing one another. The history of the common ground between Christianity and socialism is a special chapter in the road to unification. In such a union nothing would be lost and all would be saved.

Translated by Alison Weir

Notes

1. A. Gramsci, *Quaderni del carcere* (Turin, 1975), pp. 1985–86. 'Philosophy of praxis' is Gramsci's phrase for 'Marxism'.

2. A. Nesti, *Gesù socialista. Una tradizione popolare italiana* (Turin, 1974), p. 149. Tension between the Church and socialism became more serious in Italy as the Church allied itself more and more with the bourgeois against socialism when faced with 'subversive' elements which were associated with socialism in the eyes of the bourgeois state. Cf. A. Gramsci, *op. cit.*, pp. 2057–58.

3. A. Nesti, *op. cit.*, p. 150.

4. *Ibid.*, p. 152.

5. *Ibid.*, p. 154. The difference between the Christian precept of love, which has been rendered ineffectual in history through sentimentality, and the 'need'

which gives men drive is 'classic' and is to be found in the originators of Marxism. K. Marx–F. Engels, *Der Volkstribun*, ed. Hermann Kriege.

6. The reference to Renan is an explicit example of the 'preaching' by a socialist to the people. C. Prampolini, in A. Nesti, *op. cit.*, p. 197.

7. A. Nesti, *op. cit.*, p. 156.

8. The difference between historical materialism, which is acceptable, and a materialist vision of history exists within the group of 'intellectuals' of the socialist Christians around E. Buonaiuti.

9. A. Nesti, *op. cit.*, p. 166.

10. For an account of 'Catholic Communists' see L. Bedeschi, *La sinistra cristiana e il dialogo con i comunisti*, (Parma, 1966); Id., *Cattolici e comunisti* (Milan, 1974); M. Cocchi–P. Montesi, *Per una storia della sinistra cristiana. Documenti 1937–1945;* for an evaluation of the theory of it see A. Del Noce, 'Genesi e significato della prima sinistra', in G. Rossini, *Modernismo, fascismo e comunismo* (Bologna, 1972), pp. 563–652; G. Ruggieri, 'Fede cattolica e giudizio storico nei cattolici comunisti', in *La salvezza cristiana* (proceedings of the fourth national congress of the Associazione Teologica Italiana, Assisi, 1975), pp. 257–64.

11. *Voce Operaia* (26 Oct. 1943), quoted by L. Bedeschi in *Cattolici e comunisti*, p. 117.

12. *Il comunismo e i cattolici*, now in L. Bedeschi, *La sinistra cristiana*, pp. 128 ff. From the point of view of theory, this is the most important publication about Catholic Communists. The quotation above is on p. 201.

13. *Ibid.*, p. 194.

14. *Ibid.*, pp. 199–200. One of the chief spokesmen for the Catholic Communists makes a statement which relates perfectly well to the previously held position; according to him Italian Communists ought still to negotiate the passage of Marxism, which ought be looked upon not as 'ideology' but as an essential lesson in history; cf. F. Rodano, *Sulla politica dei comunisti* (Turin, 1975).

15. It is clear from reading a letter from F. Rodano to G. Andreotti, quoted by L. Bedeschi in *Cattolici e comunisti*, pp. 93 ff., to what extent it is an 'apologia'.

16. This is typical of the early attitude of the Vatican adopted immediately after the Liberation, which did not yet envisage a single Catholic party as a defence against the Communist danger.

17. See *Religione a partito* (Rome, 1945), pp. 45–51, which is the most interesting pamphlet from a theoretical point of view. This does not mean that Catholic Communists gave up on Christian commitment in the party: 'nor do we dispute that the idea of a worker class is an economic concept; in that way we defend liberty on economic grounds now released from previously held points of reference; the very act which organizes the working class politically becomes an educational effort towards a Christian spirit and thus a sense of justice and of charity which overrides restrictive interests' (p. 30).

18. In the following pages the references between brackets in the texts refer to reviews issued by Christians for socialism, Com e Com–Novi Tempi (CNT), followed by the date and the page reference.

19. Most of all by G. Girardi, *Cristiani per il socialismo: perchè?* (Assisi, 1975).

20. Cf. a typical expression made by the Protestant wing of the CPS: CNT, 28 Dec. 1975, p. 9. The statement by R. La Valle who, unlike G. Girardi, lays emphasis on the Gospel in the political struggle and was greatly acclaimed at the Naples conference, although it is hard to estimate numbers accurately.

21. These are taken from the manifesto of the Naples conference. It does not represent a commonly held point of view: CNT, 13 Apr. 1975, p. 5.

22. F. Belo, *Lecture materialiste de l'évangile de Marc*, (Paris, 1974). This does not imply that the CPS accept Belo as an indisputable master so much as feel that they ought to discuss what his position offers. F. Passuello in CNT, 3 Aug. 1975, p. 6.

23. B. Pascal *Pensées*, fr. 793 (ed. Brunschvig).

Gregory Baum

Canadian Socialism and the Christian Church

WHILE the European countries produced socialist parties at the turn of the century, Canada saw the creation of a nation-wide socialist party only in the Thirties, at the height of the Depression. In 1933, in Regina, capital of the Province of Saskatchewan, several socialist groups and progressive movements united to form a new national party, modelled largely upon the British Labour Party, which they called Cooperative Commonwealth Federation (CCF).[1] The various groups expressed their common socialist position in the so-called Regina Manifesto. The aim of the new party was expressed in the first paragraph. 'We aim to replace the present capitalist system, with its inherent injustice and inhumanity, by a social order from which the domination and exploitation of one class by another will be eliminated, in which economic planning will supersede unregulated private enterprise and competition, and in which genuine democratic self-government based upon economic equality will be possible.' 'No CCF government will rest content,' we read in the last paragraph, 'until it has eradicated capitalism.'

Canadian socialism, following the British model, was a pragmatic union of several radical and progressive movements. Strong in Saskatchewan was so-called 'prairie radicalism,' a populist movement created by angry farmers intent on protecting their family wheat farms against the threats of monopoly capitalism. Equally strong and often linked to populism was the cooperative movement, found in Western Canada and Nova Scotia, largely of British origin, which sought to help people to regain control and ownership of the means of distributing goods, and eventually of the means of production. The movement stood for cooperative ownership and hence for the abolition of wage labour. Its vision of society as a cooperative commonwealth gave the new party its name, CCF. Joined to these popular movements were organizations of urban workers, especially in Western Canada, who had opted for a planned economy and the public ownership of the means of production, coupled to their dedication to British constitutionalism. They were ready to engage in democratic class struggle.

The influence of Ontario on the formation of the new socialist party came from the League for Social Reconstruction, a society of socialist intellectuals, which had modelled itself after the Fabian Society of Great Britain. Involved in the creation of the new party were also Christian radicals, ministers and ex-ministers commited to the social gospel, some of whom had had themselves elected to parliament in the twenties as independent labour progressives. Finally the new party included the socialist movement of British Columbia with its strong Marxist emphasis. The new party, while pragmatic in its adherence to socialism and unwilling to define itself in theoretical terms, was greatly at odds, from the very beginning, with the small Communist Party of Canada. What the CCF reproached the Communists for was their adherence to a revolutionary programme, their quest for doctrinal purity, their despair over and hence their cynical use of British democracy, and above all their subservience to the directives of Moscow.

The CCF grew fairly rapidly in Canada. In the early forties, it looked as if the CCF were following the European pattern, where the socialist parties became the major alternatives to the government and eventually were elected to constitute the government. In 1944, the CCF had been elected as the provincial government of Saskatchewan and as the official opposition in three provinces, British Columbia, Manitoba, and Ontario. But then the forward movement stopped. After 1945 the CCF lost much of its support, the reform programmes it had recommended were taken over by the Liberal Party; and in order to join the Canadian mainstream the CCF considerably modified its socialist perspective.[2] The growth of the party did not follow the European pattern. The CCF had to be content to be a major third party in Canada, with influence but not within reach of power. At the beginning of the sixties, the CCF was joined by organized labour in the constitution of a new party, successor to the CCF, which was called the New Democratic Party (NDP) and included a wide spectrum of members, from the heirs of Canadian socialism who could not forget the Regina Manifesto to welfare liberals who wished to humanize capitalist society through a more developed social legislation. In this, I suppose, the NDP resembles the democratic socialist parties of Europe.

Why did Canadian socialism fail to travel the European road and become the alternative to the older, bourgeois parties? From a North American perspective, the more realistic question is why has Canada been able to create a socialist party while the USA never succeeded, despite several attempts, to organize a socialist party on a national scale, fully recognized in the country's day-to-day political life.[3] This question, important though it be, takes us away from the topic of this article, which is the relation of the Christian Church to Canadian socialism. Still, it is important to point out here that Canadian labour was, on the whole, not behind the CCF in the thirties and has never, not even after the formation of the NDP, wholly identified itself with the Canadian socialist party. Canadian labour has always been uncertain whether to follow the US American or the British model of the labour movement. In the USA, labour on the whole remained politically and ideologically uncommitted and voted for representatives of whatever party as long as they had proved themselves friends of labour, while in Great Britain the labour movement had identified itself quite early with a socialist party as its political arm and ideological base. Since most Canadian workers were unionized under US American auspices or at least belonged to so-called international (which means US-based) unions, the American model often seemed more plausible to Canadian workers than the British model, found in the United Kingdom and the Commonwealth countries such as Australia and New Zealand.

THE PROTESTANT SOCIAL GOSPEL

The Protestant contribution to Canadian socialism is considerable. Between 1914 and 1924 the Canadian social gospel, derived from British and American sources yet expressed in terms of the historical, social movements in Canada, inspired churchmen of various denominations, especially Methodists, to promote a radical social Christianity, to form labour churches in various parts of Canada, and to exercise leadership among the oppressed farmers and workers in the West. This period of the social gospel has been studied by Richard Allen in his important *The Social Passion: Religion and Social Reform in Canada.*[4] The Canadian social gospel was not confined to social sentiment and liberal reform. Karl Marx, we recall, called Christian socialism the clergy's remedy for the heartburn of the aristocrat. In Canada, besides the liberal form of the social gospel to which the Marxian quip might apply, there was a radical wing in the church that made common cause with the radical social movements in the country, especially the West. The social gospel created a language for rejecting capitalism and outlining the just society that must be built, a language which was used, in the early twenties, in the reports of the Committee on Social Service and Evangelism of the Methodist Church. Despite the considerable influence of radical Christians on church committees, they eventually found themselves at odds with their denominations which decided to align themselves more and more with the dominant section of Canadian society. The radical ministers and ex-ministers moved into more secular environments. Some of them were elected as independent progressives to parliament. Of special distinction is J. S. Woodsworth, formerly a methodist minister, member of parliament during the twenties, and the main founder and first national leader of the CCF party.[5] The estrangement between the churches reconfirmed in conservatism, and the Christian radicals turned secular, brought to a close the first phase of the Canadian social gospel. While it lasted, it had contributed to the social movement that eventually brought about the CCF.

In the thirties, after the foundation of the CCF, at the height of the Depression, the social gospel acquired new strength. In close association with the League for Social Reconstruction, the Canadian equivalent of the British Fabian Society, a group of Christian theologians in Toronto and Montreal began to interpret the Christian gospel in the light of a socialist analysis of society. They formed an organization, the Fellowship for a Christian Social Order, which was to exert a considerable influence on the Protestant and Anglican Churches in Canada during the thirties.[6] These theologians were not alienated intellectuals aloof from the historical movements; they were involved in the struggle of the labour movement and the CCF party, and related their theological reflections to the social conditions of Canadian life. Their work is available in articles published in various journals and in a book, *Toward the Christian Revolution*, edited by Gregory Vlastos and R. B. Y. Scott, a collection of essays on socialist theology. Through the work of the Fellowship, many Christians came to identify themselves with the Canadian socialist movement in the thirties.

The social gospel of the thirties achieved considerable theological sophistication.[7] For one, the theologians tried to integrate Marxian principles into their understanding of the historical transformation of society. Beyond that, the Canadian theologians refuted the influential neo-orthodox theology of Reinhold Niebuhr, which had successfully discredited the social gospel in the USA. Niebuhr had accused the early social gospel movement of liberalism, of underestimating the power of sin, and hence of expecting the arrival of the kingdom of God on earth. The social gospel, Niebuhr thought, neglected the radical and unfulfillable demand of the New Testament, which is selfless love, an *agape* ideal that makes sense in interpersonal relations and has no direct application in the social order. Social life, Niebuhr thought, must be based on realistic and cautious compromise. Against Niebuhr, the Canadian socialist theologians affirmed that they were not liberals, that they had a developed sense of sin, except that for them the sin of the world was mainly social and found expression in the contradictions of society. They did not expect the kingdom of God on earth. But they did regard the promise of God's kingdom as the measure by which to evaluate the contemporary social order. They, not Niebuhr, were faithful to the eschatological tension of the Gospel. Moreover, the socialist theologians repudiated Niebuhr's idea that the absolute summons of the Gospel was toward *agape* or selfless love which had no direct social meaning. For the Canadian theologians the Gospel summoned Christians to love as mutuality, an ideal that had at once personal and social meaning. It was the summons to mutuality that demanded the rejection of the economic system based on competition and exploitation.

Finally the Canadian theologians criticized the existentialism of Niebuhr. For Reinhold Niebuhr, following the existentialist tradition, anxiety was an important human datum. Personal anxiety revealed to Niebuhr the essential disunity in man and became a stepping stone to theology. The Canadian theologians felt that before such a step towards metaphysics be undertaken it is necessary to examine whether and to what extent anxiety is generated by the contradictions in society. A competitive achievement-oriented society, threatened by unemployment and other forms of insecurity, generates anguish of the soul that cannot be healed by inward faith but by Christian involvement in building a cooperative, egalitarian society. Existentialist thought, the Canadian theologians felt, avoids a critical analysis of the social base of human existence.

In the forties, the Fellowship for a Christian Social Order declined and eventually fell apart. With the waning of the socialist movement in Canada after 1945, the Christian Church became more reconciled with the mainstream of society. Today, after thirty years, there are some signs of renewed interest of Protestant thinkers in socialism.

THE CATHOLIC POSITION

The Catholic Church in Canada is made up of two sections that are culturally and socially distinct, the French Canadian Church with majority status in Quebec and the English-speaking Catholic Church with minority status in most parts of Canada. When describing the reaction of Canadian Catholics to CCF socialism, it will be necessary to distinguish between the two branches of the Canadian Catholic Church.

In the earlier part of the century, Catholics were involved in socialist movements only by way of exception. The Province of Quebec was a wholly Catholic culture with a labour movement largely controlled by the Church and, after 1921, with Catholic labour unions obedient to religious authority. In the English-speaking provinces of Canada, Catholics were involved in radical movements only in places like British Columbia and Nova Scotia where coal mines and steel works created conditions of extreme exploitation and summoned forth a labour solidarity that made religious differences irrelevant. On Cape Breton Island, at the Eastern tip of Nova Scotia, with a work force that included more Catholics than Protestants, Catholics were active in the socialist movements.

In 1933 the CCF was founded. How did the Canadian Cathloics react to the new socialist party? We recall that in 1931 Pope Pius XI, in his encyclical *Quadragesimo anno*, had condemned the moderate socialism of his day. Cardinal Bourne, Archbishop of Westminster, almost immediately made a public declaration that the papal comdemnation did not apply to the British Labour Party.[8] While there were some members in the Labour Party, he said, who held strict socialist views of the kind condemned by the Pope, on the whole the party stood in the tradition of British socialism which is built on different principles and does not fall under the papal condemnation. Catholics were free to remain in the Labour Party. The Catholic hierarchy of Australia and New Zealand took the same attitude toward the labour parties of their countries. When the CCF was founded in 1933, modelled after British socialism, the Canadian bishops did not follow the policy of the Catholic bishops in the British Commonwealth. Instead, they applied the papal condemnation of moderate socialism to the new party and warned Catholics against it.

Already in October 1933, three months after the publication of the Regina Manifesto, the Canadian national hierarchy issued a declaration on the dangers of the present hour, in which they warned the Catholic population that socialism under any form was not an adequate remedy for the grave social ills of the Depression.[9] While the CCF was not mentioned by name, the declaration warned against new parties that propose a moderate socialist programme and attract many good people by the elements of truth embedded in their position. In February 1934, the Catholic bishops of Saskatchewan where the CCF had its strongest grassroots support, published a letter in which they warned against the new party, again without mentioning it by name, which was based on principles that would ultimately undermine the Christian world order.[10] The Canadian bishops followed here the papal teaching. For according to Pius XI, moderate socialism is a political philosophy that is afraid of its own conclusions. Moderate socialism, according to the Pope, is willing for tactical reasons to play down its materialist or atheist conception of life, to limit the nationalization of private property to the essential industries, and to replace class war by political conflict according to democratic principles. In its essence, the Pope held, socialism remains atheistic, opposed to all private property, and dedicated to violent revolution. By its own bent, the Pope argued, moderate socialism leads to communism. 'No one', he concluded, 'can at the same time be a sincere Catholic and a true socialist.'

What happened in Quebec? Here the bishops condemned the CCF by name. In February 1934 Archbishop Gautier of Montreal preached a sermon, later made available to the press, in which he offered a detailed evaluation of the CCF position, referred to the Regina Manifesto, declared it to be at odds with Catholic social teaching, and forbad Catholics to join the CCF or vote for it.[11] The firm position of the bishops was one reason why the CCF never made any lasting inroads in Catholic Quebec.

There were also cultural reasons why the CCF appeared as the enemy to the Quebec population. Even the Catholic radicals associated with a movement called l'Action Libérale Nationale, who developed the anti-capitalist side of papal teaching, found it impossible to cooperate with the CCF.[12] The Catholic radicals asked for strong government to break the power of the foreign-owned companies in Quebec and to promote the livelihood of the farmers, craftsmen, and small shopkeepers in the province. They opposed the trend toward industrialization and hoped that Quebec could remain largely rural in character. Yet even these progressives could not cooperate with the CCF. The CCF favoured a strong federal government at Ottawa that could deal with the powerful corporations and initiate economic planning, while the progressives of Quebec favoured a strong provincial government that would be able to take care of Quebec's problems. French Canadians feared the centralizing trend of Canadian socialism. The CCF was based on the vision of a united Canada while the progressives of Quebec dreamt of a largely independent Quebec. Last but not least, the CCF was a secular political movement with a certain Protestant, evangelical flavour, while the Quebec radicals were staunchly Catholic. Canadian socialism then, even at its highest point, was never ar home among French Canadians.

Let us return to English-speaking Canada. Why, we must ask, did the English-speaking bishops repudiate the CCF in the thirties? Why did they not follow the example of the British Catholic bishops? It seems to me that the Catholic Church in English Canada was in a position similar to the labour movement: it was strongly US-oriented and when confronted with a choice between a British or an American model of action, it usually preferred the American one. Catholics in English-speaking Canada formed a subculture in the Protestant land and for this reason felt closely linked to the Catholics of the USA who formed a similar subculture in their country. Socially concerned Catholics in English Canada let themselves be inspired by the socially concerned Catholics in the USA, who were behind the labour movement, behind Roosevelt's New Deal, behind new legislation to promote social welfare and break the power of monopolies.[13] The socially minded Catholics in the USA were issue-oriented, they avoided political ideology and especially socialist language, and they favoured the dominant trend of American labour to remain politically non-partisan. American Catholics wanted the traditional parties to adopt social ideals and promote justice, and they hoped that these parties would be supported by high-minded and socially-concerned people from all classes of society. A labour party, based largely on a single class, was against their vision of society. It is my view that this American Catholic perspective made Canadian Catholics, especially the bishops, look upon the CCF as a dangerous movement.

It was only in 1943 that the Canadian bishops were persuaded to make a public declaration that Catholics were free to vote for any of the political parties, with the single exception of the Communist Party. Yet since this declaration did not mention the CCF by name and since some Catholic papers pretended that the bishops had not really changed their minds, the social impact of the bishops' declaration remained quite small.[14] The position of Catholics in regard to Canadian socialism is well described in the now famous letter of Father Eugene Cullinane, the first priest who publicly joined the CCF in Saskatchewan in 1945: 'The mentality of most Catholics I have met across Canada, including the clergy, is affected by a terribly distorted view of the CCF reality. The result is that Catholics generally are afflicted with a deep-rooted though unconscious prejudice against the CCF . . . Catholics by and large condemn the CCF for what it is not; they are enslaved by the tyranny of a single word—'socialism.'[15] The influence of Catholic teaching and the impact of American culture prevented the Catholics in Canada from distinguishing between various kinds of socialism and allying themselves, as did their co-religionists in England, Australia and New Zealand, with a British socialist party.

The socialist movement in Canada did not follow the European pattern. It did not become the main alternative to the bourgeois parties and eventually constitute the government. One of the reasons for this, as we mentioned above, was the US-American orientation of Canadian labour. Another reason is undoubtedly the opposition to the CCF on the part of the Catholic population of Canada, which constituted a majority in Quebec and a significant minority in the rest of Canada, especially in the working class.

Let it be said immediately that there were important exceptions to the general rule. In Saskatchewan a largely Catholic farming community elected a Catholic, Joseph Burton, as CCF member of the provincial legislature in the thirties and later as a CCF member of parliament.[16] But it was mainly in the parts of Canada with mining industry and a tradition of radical unionism, such as British Columbia, Northern Ontario and Cape Breton, that Catholics supported the CCF. In Cape Breton with its Catholic majority the CCF was organized in 1938. Here Catholics participated in the socialist movement from the start. The Catholic bishop, following the British model, did not interfere. The CCF candidates campaigned among the people by citing the anticapitalist passages from the papal encyclicals. To this day, Cape Breton has retained a social awareness that differs considerably from the rest of the country. The miners and steel workers of Cape Breton continue to elect NDP representatives to parliament. Among them is Father Andrew Hogan, the first priest ever elected to the House of Commons.

Today there are signs in the Christian Church of a renewed interest in socialism. This is true especially in French Canada, a society in transition. Here the socialist vision of society is expressed largely in Marxist terms. A group of Catholics, including workers and intellectuals, called Politisés Chrétiens, is presently pursuing the meaning and power of Marxist socialism from the Catholic faith-perspective.

Notes

1. Walter D. Young, *The Anatomy of a Party: The National CCF* (Toronto, 1969).

2. G. Caplan, *The Dilemma of Canadian Socialism* (Toronto, 1973).

3. Cf G. Horowitz, *Canadian Labour in Politics* (Toronto, 1968), pp. 3–57.

4. Toronto, 1973.

5. K. McNaught, *A Prophet in Politics* (Toronto, 1959).

6. Roger C. Hutchinson, *The Fellowship for a Christian Social Order*, Th. D. Thesis (Victoria University, Toronto, 1975).

7. In the following I rely on Roger Hutchinson's Th. D. thesis, *op. cit.*

8. See *Tablet*, June 20, 1931; also cf. *Tablet*, Feb. 16, 1935.

9. Jean Hulliger, *L'enseignement social des évêques canadiens de 1891 à 1950* (Montréal, 1958), p. 192.

10. *Ibid*, p. 193.

11. *Ibid*. pp. 194–95.

12. J. Levitt, *The CCF and French Canadian "Radical" Nationalism*, MA Thesis (University of Toronto, 1965).

13. David O'Brien, *American Catholics and Social Reform*, (New York, 1968).

14. M. C. Ballantyne, 'The Catholic Church and the CCF', Canadian Catholic Historical Association, *Report* (1963), pp. 33–45.

15. The letter is quoted in S. M. Lipset, *Agrarian Socialism* (Berkeley, 1971), pp. 210–11.

16. G. Baum, 'Joe Burton: Catholic and Saskatchewan Socialist', *The Ecumenist*, 14 (July-Aug., 1976), pp. 70–77.

Víctor Manuel Arbeloa Muru and
José María González-Estéfani y Robles

Socialists and Christians:

Confrontation and Dialogue

FROM REVISIONIST SOCIALISM TO HUMANIST SOCIALISM

The first linking figure to consider is Edouard Bernstein (1850–1932).
Bernstein tried to soften the materialist concept of history by emphasizing the role played by ideological and institutional factors in historical
evolution. Defending the reciprocity of influences, he attacked the
dialectic method and its inexorable determinism, introducing liberty
and will-power as active factors in history. There is a democratic
breath blowing through all his work which contrasts with the rigid
dogmatism of Marx.

After Bernstein, the 'Austro-Marxists' grouped round Kautsky
(1854–1938) also attempted to build a democratic Socialism. Special
mention should be made of the French socialist Jean Jaurès (1859–
1914), who without denying the influence of economic factors stressed
the importance of ideas and man's voluntary action in history as something that was capable of over-riding determinism; he considered the
respect due to the human person, postulated reconciliation between the
proletariat and the middle classes, defended the concept of freedom in
the State, proposed a decentralized and syndical collectivism and tried
to reconcile internationalism and nationalism. English Fabianism is
slightly outside the scope of this article; it rejected Marxism, leaving
itself with an administrative State Socialism capable of assuring the
common good, which it defined as the maximum of happiness, equality
and security of individual and collective freedoms. Another English
socialist phenomonon, the Guilds movement, was closely linked with

23

Utopian Socialism, concentrating more on moral values and not content with the utilitarianism of the Fabians.

In Italy, Antonio Labriola (1843–1903), in his study of the materialist concept of history, stressed the will of the human spirit and the reciprocity of various very active factors throughout the course of human history as decisive factors. Arturo Labriola (1859–1904), anticipating the criticism of Henri de Man, showed that Marxism cannot give a full account of the true instincts of the masses and that it over-estimates economic necessities.

The Belgian Henri de Man (1886–1955) went further than Bernstein himself. Disillusioned by the reality of the socialist revolution, which he had personal experience of in 1917, and also by the reformist movement in European Socialism, he tried to study the motives behind these realities and devoted himself to the task of replacing the materialist concept of history with a psychological, spiritualist, voluntarist and moralist interpretation of the history of man and of humanity. He attacked the determinism, hedonism and above all the rationalism of Marxist history. Socialism for him was above all an eternal ideal which existed before the working-class movement and is enriched in historical development. Christianity played a basic role in the formation of this ideal and modern Socialism cannot be understood without taking this into account. In his Heppenheim theses of 1928 he upheld Socialism's need of an ethic taken from religion, philosophy and popular belief; he replaced historic determinism by the action of the socialist will guided by universally valid aims since, 'Socialism is a tendency of the will towards a just social order'; in the same way he rejected the narrow spirit of class consciousness, making the class struggle derive from Socialism rather than the other way round.

The French Socialist Party, in its declaration to the International Congress of Geneva in 1920, also rejected historical materialism and the class struggle which it considered as provisional elements; it defended freedom of conscience, declared itself nationalist and internationalist at the same time and opposed to any dictatorship whatever form it might take.

THE SECOND INTERNATIONAL AND RELIGION

The theme of religion and Christianity crops up from time to time, as we can see, throughout the history of European Socialism. In 1903 the review *Le Mouvement Socialiste*, published in Paris, taking advantage of the anti-clerical political climate in France, asked the socialist leaders of the Second International what the relationship between anti-clericalism and Socialism should be. The conclusions the International came to can be grouped into two categories: the attitude of Socialism of the Church seen as an economic, political and social power and the attitude of Socialism to religious beliefs and the personal feelings of individuals.

There was scarcely any divergence of opinion on the first point and all the parties seemed to be unanimous in their attitude to the Church as "institution". Paragraph six of the Erfurt programme reappears virtually intact in all the socialist programmes: 'ecclesiastical corporations . . . should be considered as business enterprises managing their own affairs with complete autonomy'; everyone is free to have his Church and his priests and to defray their expenses just like any member of a cultural group or sporting club; the State should not intervene in all this. Consequently everything that gives the Church an official character should disappear. The question of religious orders is somewhat more relevant: the basic conclusion was that they should enjoy the same freedom of association as socialists would demand for themselves. The French Party was the only one to dissent from this view.

As for the attitude socialists should take to religion, the majority of those questioned were not in favour of the Party extending the political struggle to the moral sphere. Religion for them was a private matter. What was essential and decisive in history was the economic factor and the battle had to be fought on this field, but a distinction was made between the Party and the militants within the Party: 'the socialist principle that religion is a private affair', wrote Rosa Luxembourg, 'should not force us to absolute neutrality and abstention in religious matters except to the degree that they mean only intimate convictions and personal conscience'.

Among those who answered the questionnaire, Belfort Bax, a member of the Social Democratic Federation of Great Britain, had clear and ironic reservations to make on the principle of the private nature of religion, pointing out that dogma was far more important than the clerical elements and that therefore to fight these without bothering about dogma is attacking results without calling causes into question. H. Quelch, another member of the same Federation, seems to agree with him. Léon Furnémont, a Deputy to the Belgian Chamber of Representatives, declared that 'the free-thinking movement, the struggle against religious prejudices, favours the progress of the socialist idea', and that the continuation of religious feeling was 'the main obstacle' to overall acceptance of the programme by the proletariat, although he later showed himself against any violent action to eradicate religious feeling.

All were in favour of a clear distinction being made between bourgeois anti-clericalism and socialist anti-clericalism, however difficult it may be for the reader to see the differences between the two.

Rosa Luxembourg saw confusion between the two as more dangerous than 'the obstacles to be feared from reactionary elements in the Church'.

Bernstein, who was a friend of Engels and collaborated with him in the Erfurt programme, recalled that Engels had said nothing about the attitude the party should adopt to religion and various concepts of the world and of life, but that the spirit of the programme implied that German Social Democracy was in favour of science, 'against concepts based on supernatural revelations, biblical or other'. However, in fields where not even science would dare to say the last word, 'the party does not lay down any absolute rules for consciences'.

The majority of socialists of this generation reckoned that the religiosity of the masses would not completely disappear except with the disappearance of modern society, when man instead of being dominated by the social process would consciously direct and dominate it. Therefore—concluded the orthodox Spanish socialist Pablo Iglesias—'to stir up the proletariat to direct its activity and energy against the clergy rather than against the land-owners is the gravest error into which those who aspire to do away with human exploitation can fall'. Kautsky went further still and, largely following Engels despite the hostile attitude of the Church to any revolutionary movement, declared that this did not in any way mean, 'that it is impossible to be at once a Christian with faith and a convinced socialist democrat'. Christianity produces so many attitudes and has passed through so many social transformations while adapting itself to these that the notion of a Christian is now extremely vague and can be understood in a way that accords with socialist tendencies. The North American socialist A. M. Simons took a more concordant view still, 'a large number of socialists are atheists and materialists but their burning desires to find the means of liberating the masses from their poverty and hunger and from the vice and crime that stem from these are fully in harmony with the spirit of love and sacrifice shown by Him who suffered so much for humanity'. The American Protestant Pastor Hagerty gave a spirited defence of those clergymen of his time who were militant socialists and therefore in difficulty with their Churches. For Hagerty of course, Socialism was no more than an 'economic science' with which religion had no more to do than with 'bread or meat'. The English working-class leader Keir Hardie also propounded the same vein of pragmatic socialism. For him religious thought, like any other form of thought, would be influenced, broadened and purified by the wider vision brought by Socialism: 'and if as socialists we limit our activity to socialist propaganda, the religious question will resolve itself.'

The reply made by the German Pastor Goehre deserves a special mention. A member of the Social Democrat party and of a free Christian community based on science and solidarity, he understood materialism in the sense in which Engles understood it, and invoked Spinoza's theory of psycho-physical parallellism to make the real autonomy of the spirit possible.

Summing up these various points of view, André Morizet could say in conclusion to the survey: 'it is easy to say, as the free-thinkers do every day, that Christianity is a doctrine of resignation while Socialism claims to emancipate men. It is less easy to prevent facts being what they are and to deny the name of socialists to men who, as fervent and practising Christians, are to be found among our best militants'. Morizet also quoted a recent statement by Jaurès: 'I cannot pass over the allegations in clerical papers without protest: they present us as fanatics of irreligion, while I believe it would be horrible and a disaster to suppress the religious aspirations of the human mind. I absolutely do not believe that natural and social life are sufficient to man; we want man to be able to raise himself up to a religious concept of life, through science, reason and freedom. I do not hesitate to recognize that the Christian concept is a very high form of religious feeling. The time has come when democracy whould not seek to erase or outrage the old beliefs, but should look for what is lively and true in them, for what can remain in a freed and ennobled human conscience'.

THE BAD-GODESBERG PROGRAMME

We often tend to forget the breach opened in Marxist orthodoxy by European social democracy and its decisive importance for later developments. The Marxist-Christian dialogue really did no more than deepen and widen the monologue of many early socialists. It should not be surprising that many Christians in Great Britain, Germany and elsewhere join non-Marxist socialist parties or heterodox Marxist ones and that they defend their choice eagerly even if somewhat shamefacedly. The encyclical *Qudragessimo Anno* (May 1931) was also directed against them but its outright condemnation of any form of Socialism—which it at least distinguished from Communism—could do no more than staunch the flow of the unstoppable movement for a short time.

After the Second World War the fact that thousands of Christians had taken part in resistance movements, in the fighting itself, or had found themselves in concentration camps, made meetings much easier and more effective. In France and Italy, many Christians felt attracted to the powerful and clever Communist parties in these countries which had led the Popular Front against the enemy. Pius XII's inopportune condemnation of Communism in 1948 dealt a harsh blow to the growing movement of collaboration which was still a long way from any ideological assimilation. But it was powerless to suppress the vitality of a historical phenomenon that was to come to fruition twenty years later.

The members of the Socialist International became more and more entrenched in their earlier positions. In 1951 and in the Frankfurt Declaration of Principles, the Socialist International regarded Marxism as one of its sources of inspiration and one method of analysis, neither more nor less: 'Socialism is an international movement that requires no rigid uniformity in its conceptions; whether socialists base their convictions on Marxism or on other methods of analyzing society or whether they base them on religious or humanitarian principles, all are fighting for the same end: a system of social justice, a better life, freedom and peace'.

Conceived as the development of democracy brought about in freedom with a plurality of parties and the active participation of the people, 'Socialism aspires to go beyond the establishment of a new economic and social order. Economic and social progress find their deep moral justification in the extent to which they serve the emancipation and dignification of the human person'.

One more step and we reach the so-called Bad-Godesberg Programme approved in November, 1959 in the Extraordinary Congress of the German Social Democratic Party by three hundred and twenty-four votes to sixteen. In a language that owes little to Marxism but is strongly marked by liberal humanism and a strong dash of anti-Communism, the moral and economic aspirations are now reduced to: 'eliminating the privileges of the ruling classes and bringing all men to freedom, justice and well-being'. Private ownership of the means of production has a right to be protected and stimulated, 'provided it does not stand in the way of the organization of a just social order'. In the section of the 'basic values of Socialism', we read that 'freedom, justice, solidarity and mutual obligation derived from common solidarity are the basic values of socialist thought'; that democratic Socialism, 'which in Europe is rooted in the Christian ethic, in humanism and in classical philosophy, has no wish to proclaim ultimate truths, not from incomprehension of or indifference to ideologies or religious revelations, but out of respect for decisions made by man from faith on which neither a political party nor the state has the right to pronounce'. As for religion and the Church: 'Socialism is not the successor to religion, the Social Democratic Party respects the Churches and religious associations, their special mission and their independence'. Furthermore:

'the German Social Democratic Party is always ready to collaborate with Churches and religious associations in freedom and equality. The Social Democrat Party is pleased to note the fact that there are men whose religious adherence leads them to affirm their obligation to social action and their responsibilities in society'.

Even a socialist party like the Spanish one, perhaps the most anti-clerical and a-religious—if not downright anti-religious—of all, let itself be influenced by the preceding texts and so in its declaration after the Congress held in August 1967 in Toulouse broke with an old tradition going back to its foundation in 1879 and recognized the new directions in the Catholic Church, particularly those that stemmed from the Council. In its definition of its position it set out 'humanitarian and even religious principles', together with those based on a 'dialectical logic', as suitable means for analyzing man in his social relationships. For the Spanish socialists, 'Marxism is a method of social analysis based on dialectic, a procedure for seeking out the truth and proclaiming it, but it is not a system nor can it be a political programme; it is a vehicle and a path for reaching truth, but it is not truth in itself'. Socialism is lay, and does not tie its doctrine and action to the transcendent, but at the same time it is not anti-religious. There are ethical, moral and even ideological reasons which neither socialists nor Catholics can forget or evade since they have a common root in the consciousness of common human nature: 'Socialism and religion do not imply a neutral contradiction. The Christian Churches recognize the need for social reforms. It is not true that there has to be a Manichean division between one atheist and materialist world and another religious and spiritual one. There is no conflict between faith and lack of faith but only between exploiters and exploited. Socialism and Christianity, insofar as this is a religion of love of one's neighbour, are absolutely reconcilable.'

LIGHT AND SHADOWS OF THE CHRISTIAN-MARXIST DIALOGUE

This sort of democratic Socialism, far removed from Marxist dogma, was obviously not going to give too many headaches to Christians. In Eastern Europe, on the other hand, in the 'People's Democracies' with their single Marxist party and single ruling ideology, believers were submitted to a far harder trial. Outstanding among the small minorities who preached practical rather than ideological collaboration between Christians and Marxists was the Polish group 'Pax', which set out to bring the Catholic Church and the Communist Party closer together so that the Party would admit a plurality of ideologies within Socialism and the Church accept the social and economic elements of the system; while its efforts have not produced very encouraging results, neither have they been entirely in vain.

In the West, John XXIII's encyclical *Pacem in Terris* gave rise to a more favourable set of circumstances. The Italian Catholic journalist Mario Gozzini organized a series of meetings between Catholics and Italian Marxists to discuss the document. In the same year, 1974, the Yalta Memorandum—which was a sort of testament by the Italian Communist leader Palmiro Tolgliatti and a famous text that opened up a new era of Communism—the author recognized that, 'the problem of religious conscience, its content, its roots in the bosom of the people and how these can be supplanted should be posed in a different way from that taken in the past if we are to gain access to the religious masses and be understood by them. If not, what happens is that the hand of friendship we hold out to Catholics will be interpreted as mere expedience and almost hypocrisy'.

These were the years of debates, of seminars, of meetings. The *Paulusgesellschaft* Foundation organized meetings in Salzburg (1965), Chiemsee (1966) and Marienbad (1967). From 1967 onwards, Christians took part in the 'Weeks of Marxist Thought' in Paris and Lyons, and Marxists attended seminars of Catholic intellectuals in Paris. The same sort of thing happened all over the place. The meetings were not attended by Soviet representatives nor by representatives from those countries whose dogma remained faithful to the ruling orthodoxy of Moscow. On the other hand, there was an abundance of Italian, French, Polish and Czech Communists and these were the years of influence of Garaudy, Lombardo Radice, Mury, Luporini, di Marco, Machovec and others.

Enough has already been written about these dialogues. There is no doubt that in their time they marked a significant advance in the direction of mutual welcome and understanding between two worlds that had previously been separated by an abyss. Both sides showed themselves ready to enter into a dialogue with the other; the need for pluralism in one world and the other was recognized; there was a new valuation of the religious fact, which was seen not to depend only on the infrastructure of the people; the possibility and desirability of collaboration between Marxists and Christians in a common struggle against social injustices was recognized, there was a common faith in man.

At the same time the difficulties of dialogue once these first steps had been agreed became apparent. The meetings themselves were for many the beginning and the end of the dialogue. From time to time there was 'some desertion by Christians in the direction of the other half (and not the other way)'.

Then, some Christian critics, led by Mounier and other prophets, said loud and clearly what many progressives were forgetting: 1. that Christianity is not a dialectical vision of reality: as opposed to the Hegelian scheme the God of the Christians is a creator God, a personal and transcendent God to whom we pray because we believe in him and from whom we learn that he is our Father; 2. that the mediation through which the message is spread is also very different in the Christian and Marxist concepts: for Christianity, brotherhood exists because there is a fatherhood, and reconciliation is a means toward collective celebration of the presence of the Father; 3. that this world is not a vale of tears but neither is it paradise on earth; 4. that man has both a history and an intra-history and that the former is sometimes a passage towards the latter, etc.

VARIOUS REVOLUTIONARY POSITIONS

The dialogue soon came to seem sterile to another group of critics, but for different reasons: these critics were self-styled revolutionaries and held that if the Christians who took part in the talks were not at the same time revolutionaries, their agreement could only be superficial and formal since different projects for man and society could only be approached from totally opposed points of view and that would be the end of the matter.

In Latin America, and particularly the southern part of the continent, there were the first signs of movements that went beyond dialogue. Their members called themselves Marxist and Christian at the same time and began to summon Christians to a socialist crusade. This movement is dealt with elsewhere in this number and I do not propose to dwell on it. What is clear, however, is that in Europe little more has been done than repeat what has already been said in Latin America, and little more tried than what has already been achieved there, with perhaps the difference that the doctrinal outlines of such a commitment have been somewhat clarified. Giulio Girardi is the writer who has most clearly traced the course of this development.

As opposed to non-revolutionary Christian attitudes, which are essentially ones of polemic and dialogue—the defensive phase and the missionary phase—, revolutionary Christians no longer think of Marxism principally for pastoral or religious reasons but for political ones; they no longer regard it as atheism but as a theory of revolution. According to their various political colourings these Christians can be:

1. Christians who take up *Marxism as humanism*, more or less utopian, considered as a common root of a potentially common action
despite later philosophical and religious divergences. Many Christian
militants in Marxist parties belong to this group, which sees in the
practical and at the same time utopian Party programme a translation of
the beatitudes of the Gospel into political terms.

2. Christians who take up Marxism as a *scientific theory*. This group
considers that all philosophical debate with Marxism is outdated or in
course of becoming so and they cling on to Marxism as something valid
for their everyday experience. They would take Althusser as the in-
terpreter who suits them best. Many Christians hold this view, particularly those who are very active militants in Communist and Marxist
socialist parties. The group could also be extended to include members
of Social Democrat parties who understand Marxism rather as a
method than as a strictly scientific theory.

3. Christians who take up Marxism as a *scientific and philosophical
system*. These would regard it as capable of distinguishing between the
philosophical   truths   implied   in   scientific   theory   and   those
developments that go beyond it. Amongst them, some would consider
that Christian faith transcends every political project and all human
culture—faith as 'an eschatalogical reserve' and 'critical function'—
while others would consider that the absolute of faith can also be
reached through the relativity of temporal options. They would therefore question Christianity and the Church as fundamentally as possible,
though still recognizing the rationale that belongs to politics and the
relative autonomy of the religious sphere.

Girardi also notes that the different approaches taken by Christians
to Marxism stem not only from the nature of their political commitment
and their way of understanding Christianity, but also from the type of
Marxism they take up and the various revolutionary strategies which
the parties to which they belong are carrying out. So, for example,
there are some who follow the strict 'orthodox' Soviet line, those who
follow the Chinese line, the Trotskyites, the 'New Left', which is
everywhere apparent as a radical reply to the centralism and bureaucracy of traditional Marxism, etc.

CRITIQUES OF CHRISTIANITY AND OF HISTORICAL MARXISM

If there is one factor common to all the speeches and documents of
the Christians for Socialism movement it is their basic criticism of the
Church and the historic form of Christianity that they have experienced, coupled with an equally radical critique of capitalism. This is

done either on the level of scientific analysis, which includes analysis of the Christian religion as a social phenomenon, or on the level of striving for the alternative of a classless society, in the strategy of struggle, or on the level of revolutionary morality. But these questions are seldom studied in depth and this seems to be one of the main tasks facing these groups. At the same time, although not often sufficiently seriously, all stress the conflict between Marxism and Christianity with regard to the existence of God, whose non-existence is a baisc Marxist tenet which makes difficulty of understanding both widespread and radical.

But while some would leave this basic conflict to be solved in the course of events without bothering too much about its gravity, the more serious among them—and they make up the great majority—concentrate on clarifying the dialectical relationship between two overall systems. This dialectical relationship is only possible if both Marxism and Christianity are regarded as dynamic thought systems capable of being submitted to question and of continual renewal far removed from scholastic ossification. This supposes supplanting the 'spiritualist' and 'supernaturalist' concepts of Christianity, recognizing human values and the project of liberation as the criteria for interpreting the Christian message, while faith—which cannot be reduced to this project—confers a new meaning on both life and history, projecting them on to a very different horizon. At the same time this dialectical relationship involves a serious criticism of Marxism as a historical achievement and a profound re-thinking of some of the basic theses of the Marxist *corpus* which have until now been considered unchangeable: an affirmation of the autonomy of historical materialism—broadly understood—as a scientific theory related to all ontological materialism, and a humble dismantling of the Marxist thesis of atheism as superfluous and rejected by historical verification. Girardi sums up in the following words: ''In a period of secularization, a theory of revolution needs to affirm its autonomy, not only in relation to religion, but also for analagous reasons in relation to atheism. Only a secularized Marxism which supersedes religious discriminations can now set itself forward as the theory proper to a revolutionary party.'

Some of these Christians seriously wonder what sort of Christianity one impregnated by historical materialism would be and what would become of the unity of the Church and the continuity of its message. The official Church has said often enough that this would be a degradation and ultimately an annihilation. At the same time many orthodox Marxists—some may not say it but they do think it—state in the same way that the sort of Marxism these Christians dream of would no longer be Marxism and that these Christians are not Marxists—the best that can be said of them is that they try to assimilate only the most positive aspects of Marxism. We are perhaps here entering into a semantic tangle that it is not the business of this article to attempt to unravel.

Translated by Paul Burns

Bibliography

J.-M. González-Estéfani y Robles, *Essai sur les mouvements sociaux contemporains: le socialisme humaniste* (Madrid, 1967).
————, *Mesianismo y Secularización en los movimientos sociales contemporáneos* (Madrid, 1969).
Carlos Díaz, *Personalismo obrero* (Madrid, 1969).
————, *Hombre y dialéctica en el marxismo leninismo* (Madrid, 1970).
Ricardo Alberdi, 'Sobre al carácter científico del marxismo', in *Iglesia Viva 37* (1972), pp. 39–55.
Victor Manuel Arbeloa, *Anticlericalismo y socialismo* (Madrid, 1973).
————, 'Posiciones políticas ante el Cristianismo y la Iglesia', in *Pastoral Misionera* 8 (1975), pp. 725–41.
'Cristianos por el Socialismo', monograph issue of *Iglesia Viva,* 52–3 (1974), containing the article by Giulio Girardi, 'Los cristianos de hoy ante el marxismo', pp. 325–55.
Cristianos por el socialismo: Documentación (Estella, 1976).

Philippe Warnier

The Catholic Hierarchies of Western Europe and Socialism

THIS contribution does not in any way claim to be exhaustive, or scientific, or neutral (whether in the political or theological sense). I am not a theologian nor an expert in ecclesiology or church history. Nor am I primarily a politician. My position is that I am mainly in charge of an adult education movement with a personalist, Christian and socialist slant. As such, I am trying to help militant left-wing Christians who, in their attempt to sort themselves out, need to take into account the political dimension of their church membership and the religious significance of their political struggle.

Being myself a politically militant member of the French Socialist Party, I am convinced that in France and Europe Christianity as an existing fact constitutes an important, and perhaps even decisive, political issue.

Within the Church of France I happen to be a leader of a number of Christians who in their lives see an intimate link between their belief and their socialism and who feel that they are basically at one with the Catholic Church and yet in conflict with it. I try therefore to show my brothers in the faith that we live today in a historical situation which displays a profound correspondence between socialism and the demands made by the gospel, without, however, simply reducing the latter to the former.

Because of my nationality and the reality of the socialist movement in Europe I shall obviously rather concentrate in this article on the attitude of the hierarchies in what is conventionally designated as southern or Latin Europe, namely, those of France, Italy, Spain and

Portugal. I hope, nevertheless, not to lose sight of the others. I am also taking the liberty to take the concept of socialism in a rather broad sense. One cannot really talk about the attitude of the Western European bishops without having a close look at the theology which they proclaim and the reality of the capitalist society which the socialists attack.

We have also to look at the question of Marxism because many important socialist parties use it as one of their basic social theories. Nor can we by-pass the attitude of the bishops towards a number of ethical problems where the socialists take a different line. Finally, we cannot ignore in the process the points where some social practice of the churches (the way in which they organize social relationships themselves) agrees with the projects which socialists pursue with regard to the political organization of society.

One last word to clarify the limits and problems dealt with in this article. I am convinced of both the legitimacy of a political analysis of what the Church proclaims, and also that in the faith and as a believer, I must accept the bishops' reply in a spirit of fraternal dialogue, query again my own convictions, and criticise my own political conduct.

What I am trying to do now is:

1. to describe the different national situations which condition the bishops' attitudes towards socialism and prompt them to pursue different strategies;

2. to examine critically the topics which most hierarchies share with regard to politics and socialism, and to show that while these topics are religious, they are *also* (without being exclusively so) of an ideological nature. In other words, whatever the sincerity of the bishops, the political options are in no way neutral;

3. to suggest some positive ideas about the questions which socialist Christians may well ask themselves, starting from the declarations made by the bishops.

DIFFERENT SITUATIONS AND DIFFERENT STRATEGIES

To start with, one can suppose that the attitude taken up by the bishops is influenced by various economic, sociological and political factors. There is the degree of concentration and modernisation of capitalism; the attempt to involve the working class in a social consensus—or the lack of it; the livelihood or absence of it among pre-capitalist social strata (particularly the peasants); the presence or absence of a powerful Communist party; the question whether the socialist parties aim at a reformist improvement of the capitalist system or at a revolutionary transformation of society, and their acceptance or rejection of Marxism; the existence, absence or weakness of political forces which explicitly claim to be based on the Church's social teaching; the presence or absence of Christians who belong to a left-wing party.

The strictly ecclesiastical factors are no less important: does Catholicism represent the religion of the majority or are there Protestant churches? Is Catholicism still an 'Established Church' on the basis of a concordat or are Church and state definitely separated? Are the relations with Rome easy or difficult? What is the state of religious practice and how deeply are the churches embedded in the social structures? All this shows how different the problems are and how varied the strategies which the churches can pursue. Taking only a few examples one might put forward the following hypothesis.

Among the Germanic, Anglo-Saxon and Scandinavian nations monopolistic capitalism has reached a very advanced state. Agriculture is industrialized and the commodity trade increases its hold on every sector of social life from day to day. The class struggle has certainly not disappeared and can even be quite sharp but it aims mainly at a better redistribution of the fruits of growth and more security for the workers. The integration, however, of these workers in the social consensus dominated by an advanced capitalism has become an accepted fact. The social-democratic parties no longer question economic liberalism. In these societies the Christians work perhaps more in conservative, particularly Christian Democratic groups and (in Germany, for instance) the clergy may well support the right, although discreetly. There are also Christians among the Social-Democrats but, apart from some minority groups of the extreme left, revolutionary socialism is no problem for churches partly tied up with the social *status quo:* the problem is not sufficiently alive for that. As is evident from various episcopal declarations (in Germany, England, Switzerland, etc.), the difficulties are rather concerned with matters of sexual ethics, such as contraception, abortion, divorce, etc., where the Christian conscience objects more strongly to a certain social and moral liberalism (which may be just as much defended by right-wing liberals as by social democrats) than to one or other tendency towards socialism. One should also mention the often very lucid and courageous declarations made by the bishops of these countries on the demands of the Gospel in connection with international problems, justice towards the peoples of the Third World, the arms trade, etc.[1] Here the barely veiled criticism of the imperialism embodied in the multinational corporations joins the analyses produced by the socialists, even if it does not go so far as a worldwide attack on imperialism at large. Lastly, we must add that in countries where the churches control a powerful network of institutions (schools, mass media, etc.) the defence of these situations plays an important role in the political attitude of the hierarchy.

In southern Europe the situation is very different. There the growth of monopolistic capitalism is less advanced and the economic and social structures are more primitive. The fact that there is still a peasantry of massive importance, the revolutionary tradition of the working classes, the memory of bloody conflicts with the bourgeoisie, the deep traces left behind by the fascist régimes (the social basis of which lay in the middle classes who felt themselves threatened by capitalism), and the power of the Communist parties make one realize that the arrival of a socialist society which has broken with capitalism constitutes a possibility, more or less remote according to the situation. This is the problem which besets the churches that are essentially tied up with the social and political *status quo* but slowly begin to revise their attitude, forced by a militant laity and a youthful clergy who have opted for socialism. In such a situation the bishops see the struggle against Communism as the crux of the matter.

In Portugal a conservative hierarchy, relying on the important middle class and a number of small landowners, is clearly on the side of the counter-revolutionary forces, takes part in the anti-Communist crusade (cf. the archbishop of Braga during the summer of 1976) and has condemned the 'Marxist' and 'lay' parties, from the Communist party to the popular democratic party. In Spain a powerful fringe of the hierarchy, definitely conciliar in spirit, condemns the excesses of Francoism, supports the process of democratization set going by the King and is based on a modern Spain plainly involved in a capitalistic development. In Italy, the weakness of the socialist party, the rise of an Italian Communist party which represents one-third of the electorate and which has a social basis in every social class, coexist with a Christian democracy which is, all at the same time, powerful, discredited and incapable of arresting the economic and political decline of the country. The Church, which, in this country, represents a powerful social element, has lost the battle about abortion, openly supports the Christian Democrats and makes resisting the Communist peril the key of its policy. It is, however, faced with the fact that Christian commitment is growing within the Communist party.

In these three countries an arrangement based on a concordat or the statutory establishment of Catholicism as the state religion are the framework within which the bishops take up the cudgels in defence of the Church's institutions and the social power attached to these institutions, or, occasionally, as in Spain, try to break up this solidarity between the Church and a social order of which the injustice is only too evident.

Without yielding to a certain 'Francocentrism' the dangers of which I recognize only too well, France shows a situation which allows the bishops far more elasticity. Church and state are in fact separated; without re-arguing the causes of the situation, the criticism, based on the Gospel, of the abuses of the social and economic system is occasionally quite sharp; the fact that militant Christians are members of left-wing parties is accepted, whether people like it or not; above all, the new power of the socialist party prevents people from identifying socialism with Communism and from equating the Marxist analysis of the situation with the dialectical materialism of the French Communist Party.

Unfortunately this does not prevent certain bishops, like Bishop Elchinger of Strasbourg, from deploring the left-wing trend of Christians, and a majority of the bishops from 'defending,' the gospel against 'left-wing blockage' or from warning Christians against Marxism, identified with Communism, even when their pastoral messages rather share the dominant ideology than demand a re-examination of a capitalism, which is denounced for its abuses but not for its causes. I have rather rushed through this analysis but should not end it without mentioning that the values of democracy are now penetrating the churches in two ways. The first is the use of socialist terminology: people speak of basic communities, of self-administration, of a re-assessment of the power of the hierarchy and of rejecting the institutional dualism of clergy and laity. The second way is the use of the language of liberalism: democratization, lay participation, etc. But the progress in democracy seems to affect the Anglo-Saxon countries rather than the Latin ones (as if there was no outlet for liberating activities in the political field). Whatever the case may be, though, the hierarchies strongly uphold the idea that there is a close link between the hierarchical structure and the divine foundation of the Church.

THE MAIN ARGUMENTS OF EPISCOPAL THOUGHT

Apart from those differences in situation and strategy there is a striking convergence in the way the bishops of western Europe think. Before making any statements about socialism one might say that this way of thinking seems to deny implicitly what seems evident to all who produce a socialist analysis of society.

The themes of socialist criticism are certainly not unknown to the bishops when they denounce the abuses of capitalism. The way in which the French bishops analyzed the injustices and inconsistencies prevailing in French society in their statement *Pour une pratique chrétienne de la politique*, 1972 (Towards a Christian political practice), is significant from this point of view. And when the Catalonian bishops in their working paper for their Conference in 1974 saw in capitalism an economic, political and ideological reality based on profit and a 'materialistic and anti-evangelical doctrine', and denounced the exploitation practised by the large monopolies, they came close to a socialist analysis.

Yet, for all that, the bishops continue to treat the violence of the exploited and that of the exploiters as if it was the same; they refuse to admit that there is a class struggle; they appeal to their co-operation for the sake of the common good or even—as happened in Germany before the elections of October 1976—defend 'natural inequality' and the respect for private property. They pretend to criticise liberal capitalism and Marxist collectivism equally, treating them simply as abstract systems without in any way analysing the social forces operating in the present situation. They pretend to be outside the situation, to be above it, and advocate a 'third way' which is a myth without any historical, social or strategic substance. They preach the autonomy of temporal matters, pluralism, maintain that Christians have a freedom of option, and that it is not the task of the church to propose a model for society. This, again, does not prevent them from upholding the idea of some 'Christian' concept of democracy (Portugal, Italy) and maintaining the idea that the Church has a social doctrine by which it can judge historical situations and achievements as from outside. On the contrary, in spite of some timorous observations on the lines taken by the French bishops in their statement *Libération humaine et Salut en Jésus-Christ* (The Liberation of man and Salvation in Jesus Christ, published in 1975), they don't seem to realize that their way of thinking is ideologically conditioned. And when it seems to them that the situation is becoming critical for the social order which they uphold while criticising it, they don't hesitate (as in Portugal, Italy, and even in France) to point out in a more or less transparent way which parties the faithful must not vote for or at least to warn them against those whose 'ideology' might be contrary to Christian teaching.

When they take a stand on the question of socialist tendencies, the bishops generally take the position which John XXIII took in his *Pacem in terris* (a distinction between historical movements and the philosophical context in which they sprang up) and taken up again by Paul VI in his *Octogesima adveniens*. They insist on the various kinds of socialism today and admit that Christians can legitimately take the socialist line as long as it respects the basic rights of the human person, and this includes religious freedom. One may, however, point out that this opening up of the debate is the result of years of struggle by militants who were committed to the left before the magisterium approved of it.

But in general the bishops' attitude is unfavourable to such groups as 'Christians for Socialism' which, after the meetings in Santiago (1972) and Quebec, have spread throughout the world, especially in Italy, Portugal and Spain. They blame them for obstructing the gospel by their partisanism (as if an episcopal statement is itself politically neutral!), for applying a political analysis to the Church, and for identifying the liberation of man with salvation in Jesus Christ.

They also object to the Marxist analysis, made by such Christians, of society and the Church—an analysis which they see as inseparable from atheistic materialism.

It is precisely this problem of Communism and Marxism which colours the bishops' attitude towards socialism. In northern Europe social democracy is no longer Marxist and anti-Communism is given a concrete expression. After an undeniable denunciation of religious persecutions, Cardinal Hoeffner (German), for instance, devoted a pastoral letter to the 'persecuted brethren' of Eastern Europe in which he identified Marxism with persecution but without any mention at all of the odious repression of Christians (including bishops and priests) practised in Latin America in the name of anti-Marxism.

But in southern Europe the socialist involvement of Christians who reject the philosophy of atheistic materialism but accept a Marxist analysis, or are even Communist party members (particularly in Italy), create formidable problems for the bishops. Whether the bishops indulge in practical prohibitions (as happened to Christian Communist party candidates in Italy) or prefer exhortations of a religious nature (the French bishops told Christians that they could co-operate at the level of justice but could not subscribe to the ideologies held by 'parties' and supposed to be incompatible with the faith), the intellectual approach remains the same: Marxism is identified with the Communist organization and with dialectical materialism as an atheistic philosophy. As such it is absolutely incompatible with Christianity. It becomes even slightly comical when, for instance, French bishops, like Mgr Matagrin, call Mr Marchais to the rescue in order to establish this incompatibility once for all, or when the Portuguese bishop Ferreira Gomez speaks ironically about the 'crypto-Marxism' of Christians who try to put forward another interpretation of Marxism.

SOME LESSONS FOR SOCIALIST CHRISTIANS

Producing a political analysis of the bishops' way of thinking and showing that this way of thinking is to the advantage of the prevailing ideology does not necessarily mean a refusal to accept their statements as coming from brethren in the faith whose pastoral mission it is to serve the truth of the gospel and the unity of the Church.

Christians who live their faith in the battle for a socialist society will do well to examine themselves in the light of certain statements made by their pastors. Among many other points there are four that deserve to be spelt out briefly and to be remembered. First of all, the bishops' insistence on the danger of reducing faith to politics and Christian salvation to the various liberations of man, of identifying the Gospel with a particular political project, is a matter for fruitful reflection. The bishops have a right to be listened to when they ask left-wing Christians not to sacralize their struggle for socialism and when they talk about the faith as having a critical function. This function must make Christians accept that there are still other things with which they must break, and it opens up an indefinite space of creative freedom. It must break down the walls of certainties too easily asserted and open them up to an acceptance of the absolute, which is God.

Secondly, the bishops' constant reference to the common good, to fraternal co-operation among men, to the reconciliation of classes and peoples, to the love and the peace of the Gospel (beyond the ideological function of these themes in support of the social *status quo*) can be re-interpreted by Christians in a way which does not exclude conflict, nor the class struggle, nor revolution, nor the seizure of power. Christian socialists can only live their struggle in love, as a prefiguration of a brotherly reconciliation among all men.

Thirdly, when the bishops denounce the rejection of the reconciling function of the church, they again should be listened to. The absolutely legitimate criticism of the Church's ideological way of thinking must not become a negation of its divine mystery, nor develop in practice an attitude of hostility or contempt.

The ambiguous notion of 'pluralism' can be re-examined at new cost by the Christian socialists: it may mean the wearing but brotherly confrontation among communities that do not have the same social practice, nor, in spite of their common reference to Jesus Christ, the same faith. Although given by the Spirit, the unity of the faith must still be built up. We have to face it: we are Christians for whom the class struggle implies opponents, not enemies.

As long as the bishops do not pretend to be politically neutral they may well be the ministers of this unity which must be built up. Finally, while one can blame the bishops for wanting to identify Marxism with a particular Communist implementation and atheistic materialism, one can be grateful to them for insisting on the fact that the Marxist analysis (historical materialism) is closely linked with dialectical materialism. It is a pity that a fair number of left-wing Christians tend to ignore this difficulty and to develop a kind of schizophrenic conscience or, which is just as bad, throw the essence of their faith overboard along the way.

A basic theoretical re-examination which would extract the elements of a fresh interpretation from the formula of historical materialism and its link with atheistic dialectical materialism would today appear to be one of the most urgent tasks for all Christians claiming to be socialist.[2]

Translated by T. Weston

Notes

1. See, for instance, the statement by the Commission of Justice of the English hierarchy, or that of the Dutch bishops on disarmament and the arms trade (1976), or the campaign on this topic led by the Christians in Belgium.

2. Cf. the statement of 'Vie Nouvelle' on Marxism, in the July 1976 issue of *Vers la Vie Nouvelle* (73 rue Ste Anne, 75002 Paris).

Matías García-Gómez

Catholic Social Teaching and the Class Struggle in the Latin Language Countries

THE present debate in the Latin-language countries of Europe on the relationship between 'the class struggle' and 'the social teaching of the Church' is taking place on a very radical level. It is not simply a question of asking how far the teaching of the Church allows for the class struggle, if it does so at all. Such a question has become secondary and is now hardly asked at all. It is rather a matter of questioning the viability of traditional Catholic social teaching and even the possibility of there being such a teaching. Such a questioning apparently goes beyond the subject of the class struggle, but this is not in fact the case: what is happening is that faced with the supposed condemnation of this struggle in Catholic social teaching, those who believe in the class struggle have reacted with an energetic counter-attack, applying class analysis to the Church and introducing the practice of the class struggle into the very heart of the Church. From this point of view, criticism and rejection of the social teaching (over the whole scope of its content) is seen simply as the ideological front of the class struggle within the Church.

There is no space here to go into the details of the debate; all I can do is to draw the reader's attention to some of the main lines taken in the present discussions with the accent on their methodological aspects, which are those that condition the whole debate and which are most interesting from the point of view of fundamental theology. From the pastoral point of view this debate—let us not forget it—is considered by many of its protagonists not as a simple matter of academic discussion but as a basic aspect of the struggle which is being analyzed in the discussions. For this reason I am concentrating on examples taken from those writers in the Latin-speaking countries who are having most impact one way or another on the basic confrontation, and in this way are making a strong impression on both ecclesial and political practice.

This criterion for selection should enable us to form an overall view of the main aspects of the debate and I propose to summarize the arguments of two works[7] which—without representing extreme tendencies—are sufficiently representative of the two viewpoints from which the problem is today being approached by those writers who are conscious of its real implications.[2]

THE CLASS STRUGGLE IN THE CHURCH AND RADICAL REJECTION OF ITS SOCIAL TEACHING

The first work I analyze is by Jean Guichard, in which he clearly shows his sympathy with the newest and most incisive aspects of the question. From the methodological point of view the book is written—while still being a work of Christian reflection—almost exclusively from the standpoint of a political analyst (analyzing class from an overtly Marxist view point) and its basic aim is to apply this class analysis to the Church and its 'social teaching'.

Its general line of exposition and argument can perhaps be summed up like this: he begins by establishing the need for a 'political reading of faith' (ch. 1). This leads him to the subject of the relationship between 'Church and the class struggle' (ch. 2) in which he denies the Church's claim to neutrality in the matter and even the possibility of this neutrality: 'the internal conflicts in the Church are closely related to the socio-political conflicts in society; the Church cannot understand its real situation except insofar as it consciously realizes its duties in relation to the class struggle' (p. 48). Guichard tries to prove this hypothesis by showing first of all that—at least today—it is not possible to stay on the sidelines of the 'global confrontation', since this, by the very fact of being global, also takes the form of a 'religious confrontation' (since it is a particular form of religiosity that is being confronted) and inevitably introduces the class struggle into the Church. One particular field where this situation applies is that of 'theological reflection' which is equally shot through by class conflict, with no possible way out.

The central argument of chapter three ('Religious Practices and Political Strategies') is that 'religious strategies exist in function of something else', or put in another way, that, 'a judgment and a strategy in the political order' decide 'the adoption of a particular position on the theological level' (p. 78). He defends this argument by an analysis of the Church's attitude to violence and in particular its condemnation of violence 'in any form'. He then goes on to describe the present centralist pastoral strategy of the Church which 'places it politically in a centralist strategical position' (p. 88), and shows that there is a 'political determination' behind this choice of religious strategy on the part of the Church.

In chapter four ('We Have to Make a Choice'), after a fairly detailed description of the internal logic of the two religious strategies that are presently in conflict (reformist and revolutionary), which correspond to their related political strategies, the book ends with a return to its main theme: in the first place the impossibility of avoiding a coherent choice, which has to be applied in both fields—political and religious—and in the second place a defence of the need to choose the revolutionary strategy. Such a strategy supposes a conscious entry into the class struggle (a struggle in which the Church is in any case involved even if unconsciously), not only in secular society but in the very interior of the Church. This last aspect involves both an ideological struggle and a consequent break with and battle against the Church's social teaching.

CHRISTIANS AND THE CLASS STRUGGLE

The next work by René Coste is considerably different in character, not only in its conclusions, but above all in its methodology. From the outset, he considers it necessary to co-ordinate rational analysis with theological analysis and sets himself the object of reaching, 'the most exact understanding possible of social reality and a theological investigation as faithful as possible to the dynamic proper to faith in Jesus Christ' (p. 6). The subjects he deals with directly are the class struggle in society and the attitude the Christian should take to it; only secondarily—although in sufficient detail—does he deal with the subject of the class struggle within the Church. He begins by analyzing three texts (pp. 8–16) in which he claims to find the extreme illustration of the *three positions* currently taken up in the Church with regard to the subject of the class struggle: the first defends the need for classes, opts for collaboration between them and rejects the class struggle under any circumstances (J. Daujat); the second is not totally closed to the possibility of struggle but strongly criticizes the absolute value given to it in certain dogmatic forms of Marxism (J. Girette); the third defends a class morality and absolutizes the choice of class (and the rational analysis this implies) to such an extent that this analysis itself sits in judgment on the very affirmations of the Gospel, whose morality it considers contradictory and fragmentary (M. Blaise).

Following this introduction, the two first chapters of the book are devoted to a rational analysis of the class struggle, first from the point of view of the 'non-Marxist sociological approach' (ch. 1) and then the 'Marxist approach' (ch. 2). This leads him to accept many of the conclusions of the Marxist analysis, but also to introduce important corrections and changes of emphasis, rejecting some conclusions and contributing new viewpoints. His conclusion is that Marx put his finger on the wound, but that he, and particularly later Marxism (which tends to apply analyses and conclusions to the twentieth century when they were more valid for the nineteenth), tend to reduce all conflicts to class conflicts, thereby unjustifiably simplifying a problem which, at least today, is far more complex. His main conclusion is that: 'a theory of the manipulation of the masses by energetic small groups is more basic as an objective and in-depth interpretation of the social reality than the theory of class struggle'; and furthermore that 'its application is general; it can be seen at work in the industrial capitalist nations and in the socialist countries', 'it applies as much to the under-developed countries . . . as to Communist China'. This however does not mean that the dialectic of social classes, 'which is still an essential component of social reality' (p. 59), must disappear. In his final chapters, Coste uses this rational rather than dogmatic basis for his theological reflection, devoting one of them to the Church (ch. 3) and the other to Christians (ch. 4). Note this distinction, which is important and which I shall return to in my own conclusions. Reflecting on the Church as institution (with its praxis and its 'social teaching') in relation to the class struggle, Coste recognizes the legitimacy and value of political analyses (such as that made by Guichard), even though they are made from a Marxist and class standpoint. They stress the impact made by the fact that bishops and theologians belong to a particular class, a fact that has had and undoubtedly still has repercussions in their commitments to, and compromises with, the ruling classes, and is reflected in their way of acting and speaking (social teaching). Coste is opposed only to the extrapolations and generalizations resulting from these analyses and more basically to the claim to explain the religious teaching and practice of the Church from a predominantly political viewpoint, which is no doubt suitable for uncovering mystifications, but is incapable of providing a final and definitive explanation and justification. Coste also accepts the fact (and even the inevitability) of class tensions being reflected in the Church, but is opposed to the deliberate introduction of the practices of the class struggle into the Church (pp. 81–82). 'If we wish to be faithful to the requirements of the Word of God, we are called to build a new class Church, opposed to the other class Church we reject: a Church in which all classes and social categories are willing to meet', provided they are willing to be converted together to the truth of the Gospel. This commitment to mutual conversion would be the touchstone of true unity (pp. 82–83).

In the last chapter devoted to Christians, it would seem that Coste is not totally opposed to the practice of the class struggle, provided it is not absolutized (and even more so, not sacralized) and provided it is only undertaken after a clear and critical analysis both from a rational and scientific standpoint and in the light of faith, and provided, finally, that a code of responsible behaviour in a conflict situation is worked out.

CONCLUDING REMARKS

The scope of this short review does not allow space for a personal analysis of all the factors of the debate but I should just like to make these final points:

1. Political analysis applied to pastoral action and the social teaching of the Church (including the technique of class analysis) seems necessary if one is to avoid ingenuously playing into the hands of interests that have nothing to do with the Gospel. Certain facts and historical currents—signs of the times critically analyzed in the light of the Gospel—can be a stimulus and an illumination, leading the Church to achieve a better understanding of the fact that many of the formulations and even some of the content of its traditional social teaching have to be de-ideologized and that certain aspects of the Gospel message have not been sufficiently emphasized. In this process, taking the standpoint of the poorest classes (which only partially coincides with a class standpoint as generally understood) can have a decisive influence.

2. However, if we are to avoid falling under the sway of new ideologies, the basic point of reference for any teaching, orientation and praxis on the part of the Church must continue to be the word of God critically expressed, but also bravely used, in order to interrogate the whole human condition in a critical spirit and help the human race to overcome its conditionings—including its class conditionings. To the extent that this interrogation is possible and can be expressed in different cultural contexts, a social teaching and pastoral practice of the Church will always be both legitimate and necessary. They must become—as indeed they are in the process of becoming—more explicitly theological, that is to say more particularly referred to the word of God in the source and expression of their content, which is not a function of sociological conditionings or class perspectives.

3. It is possible that one of the points in the social teaching of the Church that should be theologically rethought is its rejection of the class struggle. It seems to me that this rejection is not basically as

radical as some rather pusillanimous and over-categorical formulations might lead one to think. But the possibility of Christians accepting the class struggle can never be the same thing as an unconditional acceptance without criticism of any struggle. The new formulations will have to move from a position of rejection to one of clarification of the conditions under which such a struggle can be acceptable to Christians[3]

4. The criterion of belonging to the Church, and the key to its unity, is reference to the word of God in order to be converted to its requirements. However, in working out these requirements and in particular in deciding what are unjust structures that have to be changed and what actions have to be taken in order to change them, technical aspects which cannot always be resolved by reference to the word of God alone, nor imposed by the institution of the Church, must necessarily come into play. This can be a cause of and justify a wide divergence of opinion (and even confrontations and struggles) among Christians without their losing their common reference to what constitutes the key to their unity. In this sense the taking of sides in socio-political struggles—even taking actions on a personal basis when such are seen to be required for the sake of fidelity to the Gospel—can never be the criterion for belonging to the Church or for its unity.

Translated by Paul Burns

Notes

1. J. Guichard, *Eglise, luttes de classes et stratégies politiques* (Paris, 1972) and R. Coste, *Les chrétiens et la lutte des classes* (Paris, 1975).

2. Lack of space forbids an analysis of two more basic works by G. Girardi: *Amore cristiano e violenza rivoluzionaria* (Assisi, 1970) and *Christianisme, libération humaine, lutte des classes* (Paris, 1972). Girardi adopts a methodological approach between Coste and Guichard, though his conclusions are closer to those of the latter. The Spanish groups of Christians for Socialism take Guichard and Girardi's ideas virtually unchanged. For further information on the Spanish scene, see 'Iniciación a la reflexión sobre Fe cristiana y lucha de clases', in Fierro-Maté, *Cristianos por el Socialismo* (Estella, 1975), pp. 158–76; J. N. García Nieto, 'Fe cristiana y lucha de clases', in *ibid.*, pp. 83–109; R. Alberdi, 'Opción de clases y acceso a la verdad', in *Iglesia Viva* 60 (1975), pp. 535–57. There is a fuller bibliography in Coste, *op. cit.*.

3. Such an analysis has been undertaken by M. García, 'Diálogo con CPS acerca del diálogo Cristiano-Marxista', in *Revista de Fomento Social* 31 (1976), pp. 160–64.

Rudolf Weiler

Catholic Social Teaching and the Class Struggle in the German Language Countries

AMONG the German-speaking peoples a cross-section of Catholic social teaching shows various directions and tendencies both in content and in time. Reaction to the 'social question'[1] brought about not only a general discussion of its attitude towards liberalism and socialism but also attempts at formulating Catholic social doctrine as a social ethic with regard to the empirical social sciences and, by implication, a return to the question of social analysis. The analysis of social conflicts and their connection with social levels and social classes has to be accepted as a general problem. But the Marxist analysis, based on its particular interpretation of the class-struggle, constitutes a spécial case.

During the period of the reconstruction of Germany, between 1945 and the sixties, the explicit re-examination of natural law and the corresponding Catholic social doctrine with its theoretical social models was a necessary starting-point for the moulding of a social awareness in accordance with Christian values. One has but to think back to the way in which the constitution of the German Federal Republic was formulated. Even liberal and social-democratic movements were anxious to stress their agreement with Christian social thinking.

In the course of the years Catholic social teaching came to be increasingly preoccupied with specific issues to the point where some came to abandon the idea of a specifically Catholic social model of society[2] and of a satisfactory delimitation of ideological criticism. In particular, the years immediately following the Vatican Council saw a normative social doctrine of the Church as an obstruction to the flexibility which the encounter between Church and world required.[3] Moreover, the close of the sixties saw the rise of the major argument between Catholic social doctrine and the new political theology which had sprung up within the Catholic Church. While in this context, people like Hans Maier are struck by the fact that 'the current Marxist interpretation models are uncritically accepted'[4], O. V. Nell-Breuning claims to have caught on to the real concern with the early Marx.[5] Among the most recent developments of political theology, the South American development as liberation theology has shown itself receptive to Marx's critique of society and the idea of the class-struggle. And this has had its repercussions in Europe.[6]

This situation saw a revival of Catholic social doctrine. Outwardly this came out in the 'Katholikentag' in Mönchengladbach, 1974, the discussion on 'Catholic social doctrine' in the *Rheinische Merkur* (1974–75) and the controversial repercussions to the German bishops' synod and on the Church and the worker's condition *(Kirche und Arbeiterschaft)*. During this period the Centre for Social Sciences in Mönchengladbach (G. Gundlach and later A. Rauscher) already showed its influence beyond the German Federal Republic by way of conferences and publications as the centre for traditional catholic social doctrine. A monthly publication *Kirche und Gesellschaft* has dealt with actual issues since 1973.[7] Another publication, *Katholische Soziallehre in Text und Kommentar,* is in course of publication.

TAKING KARL MARX FOR GRANTED

Already in 1945, but especially during the late sixties, one can observe a falling back on Marx's social analysis as of particular value for the problem of the working classes. One of the main reasons for this lies in the neglect of a general theory where the social question is concerned. A symposium which took place in Vienna in the autumn of 1975 tried to contribute some clarification in this matter.[8]

When one looks at the state of modern research into crisis and conflict and considers the social and historical philosophical assumptions of this research in the light of ideological criticism, it is astonishing to see that many of those that represent Catholic social teaching do not accept this challenge of the social sciences but are content to base themselves on Marx. Yet, this kind of Marxist renaissance seems to show that today there is a link between basic trends and older currents in social teaching which can best be described as romantic and social-

realistic. And here the return to Marx and his anti-capitalism seems to be typical of the romantic kind.

A key figure in German Catholic social teaching is O. von Nell-Breuning. It is, however difficult to see exactly where he fits in, and this is not only because he has been creative for such a long time. While there are texts which clearly suggest his acceptance of the Marxist social analysis and class theory[9] there are others which seem to show that he had his own idea about the classes in the tradition of Pesch and Gundlach.[10]

O. von Nell-Breuning's discussion of the truth content in Marx's doctrine could be reduced to developments in the history of ideas where these truths play a special though not exclusive rôle: thus the increased attention paid to social change and the importance given to it with the rise of sociology and the consideration applied to the influence of social institutions and their corresponding ideological justification by political science and sociology. Where Marx has least contributed is in the matter of the development of the national economy. In the context of economic value concepts Marx's theory is today rejected and modified even by neo-Marxists and their criticism of advanced capitalism (Lenin already had to develop and correct Marx in his theory of imperialism).[11] One wonders therefore with some surprise why Marx's merit and significance has suddenly become so important for Catholic social teaching, why it is so necessary to retrieve his theory and come to terms with it, and why it is so regrettable when someone fails to pay him the respect that is due to him?[12] It was really the Austrian Communist reformist, E. Rigler,[13] who, in his review of R. Bücheler's book, *Christsein im gesellschaftlichen System* (Vienna, 1976), hit the nail on the head. Büchele was a pupil of O. von Nell-Breuning, and Rigler saw in his theses simply a 'return to traditionalism'. 'In spite of many attempts at modernization' the author could not get beyond the 'context of *Quadragesimo Anno*'. Particularly the opposition between the classes should not be taken as conditioned by the system. Without the philosophical assumption of dialectics as the law of historical progress in the sense of a kind of antagonism between opposites and their coming to an agreement, in other words, in terms of pure social analysis, there is no way of verifying the theory of the two-class system, or, exceptionally, as a useful hypothesis. Moreover, the refinement of the theory by taking into account the many reactions between basis and superstructure makes it constantly more complicated for social scientific analysis to be in close touch with the real situation so that the decision-taking where political action is concerned always remains open-ended and has to accept a moral responsibility. The Marxist-inspired solution of the conflict via the changing of the structures seems to be no longer viable. And so the Marxist analysis of the value of its political prognosis has vanished and loses its appeal.

Marx's concept of the class-system depends on the question whether social conflict is always ultimately a class-conflict is therefore exclusively rooted in the social system and can therefore only be solved on this basis. But doesn't social psychology already suggest that there are other factors at the root of the class-system than the purely economic ones? Is it therefore not possible that attempts at co-operation between the classes are viable?

Berdyaev, in his days, had already objected to the metaphysical generalisation of the class-idea in Karl Marx.[14] Today, too, the class-concept is often used as a way of social-anthropological wishful thinking based on a real background of exceptional cases in social history, which allows the social conflicts to be reduced to a simple conflict between two major groups, the 'upper' ones and the 'lower' ones, or the 'rich and the poor' or the 'exploiters' and the 'exploited'. Over against this position, the national economist Milton Friedman[15] has shown that the general forecast that, e.g., a general increase in real income makes the rich richer and the poor poorer, does not hold for individual income and wealth, as long as the individual person enjoys freedom of decision!

While even Communist parties begin to avoid the term 'class-struggle' and take it out of social practice and consign it to fundamental philosophy, we have to ask ourselves what German Catholic social teaching has to tell us about it.

THE CONCEPTS OF CLASS AND CLASS-STRUGGLE IN GERMAN CATHOLIC
SOCIAL TEACHING

Classes are counted as a feature of the so-called 'free society'.[16] N. Monzel,[17] for instance, deals with the class-concept chiefly in connection with 'social position' and, following W. Sombart, considers classes as 'merely externally coherent conflicting groupings only held together by similar economic interests'. This leads him to distinguish a class-struggle 'free from class-hatred' as a morally acceptable means of use in the labour conflict and a 'class-struggle in the Darwinian sense as understood by Marxism and individualistic liberalism'.[18] Monzel, too, appeals to O. von Nell-Breuning in defence of his point of view. J. Höffner treats of class and class-struggle in a less systematic but factually similar way.[19] The most important independent study of class and class-struggle still seems to be that of G. Gundlach[20], newly presented by J. Messner[21] and Messner's own elaborations of it.[22]

This latter author distinguishes between the destructive class-concept of Marxist theory and a constructive theory of the class problem. Class (as primarily a social group based on a community of interests) also has accordingly the right to class-struggle and class-solidarity. He sees the positive role of Marx and his class-theory as a first-rate political factor 'in the awakening of class-consciousness among the workers of the continent of Europe'. For the rest he sees Marx's class-theory in itself as 'not corresponding to the facts' and also as out-of-date in so far as the present state of this awareness is concerned.[23]

In essence F. Klüber also maintains that 'the concept of the class-struggle in Catholic social teaching must be dissociated from Marxism' and that the moral permissibility of a class-struggle must depend on whether it leads to 'the restoration of a justice which has been violated'.[24] In assessing Marx's influence on the Church's social teaching since Leo XIII and his major historical achievement, 'the analysis of the class society of the nineteenth century', he goes still further than O. von Nell-Breuning.[25]

The Christian, like the other non-Marxist, tradition in social sciences recognizes many factors which lead to the formation of classes which can be traced to *both* social influence and individual factors as the main causes. This means a clear rejection of Marx's ideas about class and the consequent theory of the class-struggle.[26] In opposition to Marxism and socialism the class-struggle as a revolutionary process, postulated by historical necessity in man's evolution and the need to achieve social justice, is not accepted. An exception is made, however, for the right to social self-defence when a large group of people cannot otherwise overcome a lasting and severe injury to the common good.[27] The conflict of interests between classes is something different, but already early on mentioned as 'class-struggle' in ecclesiastical statements.[28] We have therefore clearly to deal with terms which have different meanings. This is an incontrovertible conclusion which follows from J. Messner's most recent study[29] in so far as the social doctrine of the Church is concerned. Other attempts at interpretation appear in Catholic social teaching which Messner describes as 'unrealistic thinking', romanticism or playing with words, the main point of which might be to produce a bad conscience in Catholic thinkers on the pretext of a serious failure to deal with the question of the workers in the past. But as E. Nawroth[30], among others, has most impressively pointed out, the Catholics were ahead of Marx and didn't have to borrow from him.

In this argument with the theology of liberation, in so far as it clearly shows Marxist symptoms, Wilhelm Weber sees the fact that the acceptance of violent class-struggle is inevitable as the expression of a lack of imagination. He accuses the advocates of this theology of being disciples of Marx who put utopian assurance in the place of Christian hope. On this point Marx's class-concept is today simply unrealistic.[31]

Nobody today can intelligently look for the solution of the development problem of the Third World through the collision of North and South in Marx's analysis and expectation. The development of a solution of the workers' problem has exactly proved that the class-struggle theory of Catholic social teaching is right in so far as it has tried to overcome the split between the classes in society by reform measures and by reducing extreme class differences through socio-economic and political co-operation in the sense of social partnership.[32]

The phenomenon of a certain Marxist renaissance within Catholicism may, in the case of its supporters in the field of German Catholic social teaching, perhaps be explained as an emphatic way of speech aimed at producing a shock in order to point the need for a more effective consideration of the interests of employees.

The class-struggle ideology, however, is not a real driving force to achieve social progress. What matters today is to think about a worldwide common good, a just ordering of working conditions at the international level, and economic co-operation. To think in terms of class-struggle as the expression of a self-centred re-distribution is precisely what prevents the solution of the problems of the developing countries. What matters is the integration of the developing countries and the highest possible productivity of capital in this world in the fight against hunger. Co-operation and eliminating the class-struggle through social partnership is also internationally the quickest and most fruitful way of overcoming the crisis. The monstrous burden of armaments and the continuing armaments race are, among other things, the result of the profound mistrust which exists between East and West because of the class-struggle ideology and the consequent existence of two systems of society and peace. Since neither will disappear in a hurry international realities themselves demand a co-operation which shows the old, Marxist-loaded use of words increasingly as antiquated ballast.

Apart from forty-five years and more of interpretation of texts, and from the point of view of both intelligence and the facts of life, all signs point away from swearing by the spirit and letter of Marx's social analysis and his class-struggle model. Catholic social teaching should beware of concerning itself with old-fashioned Marxism as a refuge for antiquated theories over against modern praxis, whether it does so by playing with words or out of a false romanticism.

Translated by T. Weston

Notes

1. Cf. R. Weiler, 'Von der Dynamik der Gesellschaft', in *Zur Theorie sozialer Krisen und sozialer Erneuerung, Gesellschaft und Politik*, no. 3, 1976, pp. 7–26.

2. By way of example I refer to O. von Nell-Breuning who in the decade between the first and second edition of his article on the social question simply deleted the reference to the corporate system as a social model of Catholic social teaching, without putting anything in its place *(Wörterbuch der Politik*, part III, Freiburg i.Br., first ed. 1949, 2nd ed. 1958, p. 8).

3. Quoted by J. Giers, 'Katholikentage im Wandel von Gesellschaft und Kirche', in *Münchener Theol. Zeitschrift*, vol. 25, no. 3, 1974, p. 224.

4. 'Politische Theologie?', in *Stimmen der Zeit*, no. 2, 1969, p. 84.

5. ' "Politische Theologie" —einst und jetzt', in *Stimmen der Zeit*, no. 10, 1970, p. 239.

6. Cf. Wilhelm Weber, 'Marxismus—ein für Kirche und Theologie annehmbares gesellschaftskritisches Interpretament?', in *Kirche und Befreiung*, ed. F. Hengsbach and A. L. Trujillo (Aschaffenburg, 1975), pp. 127–39. For the growing modern left-wing trends in the Church today, see R. Weiler, 'Linkstendenzen in Gesellschaft und Kirche', in *Die Kirche im Wandel der Zeit*, a publication in honour of J. Höffner (Cologne, 1971), pp. 453–67.

7. See with reference to my theme, J. Messner, 'Klassenkampf oder Sozialpartnerschaft?' in no. 32 of the publication referred to in the text (1976).

8. *Soziale Krise—soziale Erneuerung, Gesellschaft und Politik*, no. 3, 1976, pp. 5–55.

9. Thus already in *Wörterbuch der Politik*, vol. V, 'Gesellschaftliche Ordnungssysteme, Marxismus' (Freiburg i.Br., 1951), pp. 240f. Finally, see the discussion about the saying 'we are all carried on the shoulders of Karl Marx' in *Stimmen der Zeit*, no. 9, 1976, pp. 609–22. A longer list of pertinent remarks, particularly in connection with J. Messner's disclosure of his contribution to the text of *Quadragesimo Anno*, can be found in his essay, 'Marx in der kirchlichen Soziallehre? in the publication in honour of Fritz Eckert, ed. by H. Schambeck, (Berlin, 1976), pp. 403–17.

10. In a 'Festschrift' article, 'Arbeitskämpfe', in 1973, reprinted in *Der Mensch in der heutigen Wirtschaftsgesellschaft* (Munich 1975), pp. 89–105, he writes about workers' conflicts in the social constitutional state as a necessary evil but nevertheless an honest and honourable way towards social peace (p. 105) and often distinguishes this from the class-struggle in a 'two-classes' society where no true peace is possible since there the struggle aims at the destruction of the opposing party (p. 101). O. von Nell-Breuning often suggests that in the former case we should talk about 'discussions by both classes' as they group themselves around the labour-market (with reference to *Quadragesimo Anno*). But this cannot logically be understood as a simple gradual transition from class-struggle to class-war, and must include Marx's concept of the antagonism inherent in his concept of the class-struggle. On this last point see the article, "Welcher Platz gebührt der Wissenschaft in unserem Welbild?" (1966), reprinted in *op. cit.*, p. 23.

11. See, e.g., J. Habermas, *Legitimationsprobleme im Spätkapitalismus* (Frankfurt, 1973).

12. 'Auseinandersetzung mit Marx und seiner Lehre', *op. cit.*, p. 181.

13. *Wiener Tagebuch*, no. 10, 1976, p. 22.

14. *Christentum und Klassenkampf*, 1936.

15. Cf. his hypothesis of a permanent income.

16. A. F. Utz, *Sozialethik*, pt. I (Heidelberg, 1958), p. 333.

17. *Katholische Soziallehre*, vol. 2 (Cologne, 1967), p. 232.

18. *Op. cit.*, p. 457.

19. See the basic points in the register of the omnibus volume, *Gesellschaftspolitik aus christlicher Weltanschauung* (Münster, 1966).

20. See his preliminary study in the *Staatslexikon der Görresgesell-schaft*, vol. III (Freiburg i.Br., 5th ed. 1929), pp. 383–92, enlarged and reprinted in the collection *Die Ordnung der menschlichen Gesellschaft*, vol. II (Cologne, 1964), pp. 191–219.

21. Cf. 'Marx in der kirchlichen Soziallehre?'.

22. *Das Naturrecht*, 5th ed. (Innsbruck, 1966), pp. 612f.

23. *Op. cit.* p. 618.

24. *Naturrecht als Ordnungsnorm der Gesellschaft* (Cologne, 1966), pp. 203 & 201; cf. *Katholische Soziallehre*, vol. I (Osnabrück, 1968), p. 279.

25. *Op. cit.*, p. 199.

26. Cf. both the fifth and the sixth editions of the *Staatslexikon*.

27. Cf. R. Weiler, 'Katholische Soziallehre und Revolution', in *Jahrbuch für Christliche Sozialwissenschaften*, 1969, pp. 226f.

28. For references see, e.g., O. von Nell-Breuning's 'Wir alle stehen auf den Schultern von Karl Marx', *op. cit.*, p. 622.

29. Cf. 'Marx in der kirchlichen Soziallehre?'.

30. Quoted by J. Messner, *op. cit.*, p. 415. See also E. Nawroth's clear ideological critical treatment of Marx in the *Bensberger Protokolle*, no. 11, 1975, esp. pp. 18–28.

31. *Op. cit.*, pp. 133f. In his discussion of political theology E. Nawroth reaches a similar conclusion: ' "Institutionalized" social criticism without a theory which is related to reality and constructive at the same time is just hot air and politically not viable' ('Integraler Humanismus', in *Die Neue Ordnung*, no. 1, 1975, p. 28).

32. In connection with the Austrian experiments in social partnership I may refer to R. Weiler's basic study, *Wirtschaftliche Kooperation in der pluralistischen Gesellschaft* (Vienna, 1966), and the actual description of it by A. Klose, in *Ein Weg zur Sozialpartnerschaft. Das Osterreichishe Modell* (Vienna, 1970).

Kuno Füssel

Theoretical Aspects of Class Struggle

THE existence of social classes and class conflict is not only an irrefut-
able finding of Marxism but is acknowledged in papal teaching; Piux XI
in *Quadragesimo Anno,* for example, recognizes that 'modern society is
constructed on the antagonism of class interests and hence on class
conflict'. The destructive nature of capitalism is confirmed in the social
encyclicals, which also approve the struggle of the working class for
basic needs, justice and human dignity, and express solidarity with the
exploited classes. There is always a warning against systematic class
hatred, however, and against irreconcilable enmity in the political and
economic struggle. This is where the criticism of Marxism-Leninism
comes in.

The differences between both camps do not however begin with political practice based on class division, but in the definition of the very
notion of class, and continue in the explanation of the cause of class
division and the analysis of class warfare.

The decisive consequence of the understanding of the notion of class
in Catholic social teaching is opposition to the necessity of class warfare as a systematic component of capitalism, and its reduction to a
transient phenomenon resulting from class egotism and hence the moral
decision of the individual; and also the supposition that this modified
notion of class warfare is reconcilable with a conception of a common
good which applies to all men equally as the essential basis of social
reality. Then it is possible to conceive and promote reconciliation of the
classes by common orientation to the common good, and by doing
away with specific class interests.

Most of the objections raised against Marxist class theory (abstract-
ness, over-simplification, distance from real life, anachronism) result

from an inadequate understanding of the function and logical structure of this theory, but mainly from a lack of acquaintance with the 'method of idealization and concretization of theoretical models' used by Marx in *Capital* when establishing the fundamental categories and laws of the theory.[1] That has given rise to a false theoretical controversy, and has obscured the interaction of type of theory and basis of interest. This article is an attempt to correct this basis of discussion.

LOGICAL CHARACTERIZATION OF THE MARXIST THEORY OF CLASS AND CLASS WARFARE

The Marxist-Leninist theory of class and class conflict, a basic component of historical materialism. tries to answer the following questions: *(a)* into what classes is a society divided; *(b)* what is the cause of class division; *(c)* what relation do the social classes have to one another, and what influence do they have as a result on the course of history?

Class theory therefore neither enjoys the status of an arbitrary invention or one determined by interests, nor is it a tendentious refinement of existing contradictions, but represents the scientific discovery of decisive laws whose logical structure is to be shown. Marx himself said that he did not claim to have discovered the existence of classes in modern society nor conflict between them: 'What I was the first to do, was (1) to show that the existence of classes is merely connected with specific phases in the historical development of production; (2) that class conflict necessarily leads to the dictatorship of the proletariat; (3) that this dictatorship itself is only the transition to the cancellation of all classes and to the classless society'.[2]

This statement affords four important insights:

(a) Classes and class struggle are not unchanging phenomena necessarily posited with human or social nature as such, but are themselves the products of an historical development which leads from the downfall of the classless tribal communities to capitalist class society.

(b) The most important characteristics for defining social classes are obtained by analysis of the method of production.

(c) Class warfare is not only a result but a means of ending class division and class rule.

(d) The main work of transition to the classless society is undertaken by the proletariat, since under capitalism it is the most fiercely exploited class.

The main findings of Marxist class theory, as worked out by Marx especially in the context of his analysis of capitalist society in *Capital*, are to be classed as an explanatory theoretical model. On the presupposition of a number of idealistic assumptions about the pure form of capitalism, Marx derives by logic structurally descriptive statements and laws which can be gradually reduced to concrete instances by application of the idealistic premises to empirical data.

We can use the concept of class to see how this method works, and how successful it is, by moving from the abstract to the concrete in the establishment of fundamental categories.

In the first two volumes of *Capital* Marx presents a 'pure form' of the capitalist mode of production, which relies (among others) on the following idealistic assumptions:

(a) The capitalist entrepreneur is the owner of the entire surplus value produced; (b) the members of a social category are sufficiently alike.[3]

In *Capital* we can of course find many other similar assumptions which do not have to be raised here explicitly. Marx derives from them the following law: If the assumptions under (a) and (b) above are correct, then society is divided into industrial capitalists who appropriate the surplus value, but do not produce, and industrial proletarians, who produce it, and do not appropriate it, but have to sell their labour power as a commodity (the causal explanation of class division).

From such findings Marx establishes a model of the class structure of capitalist society in its pure form. Once we have the pure form, then by modifications of the idealistic premises we can show by what laws the actual circumstances arise. Here we have, for example, to introduce the modified premiss that the industrial capitalist has to share the surplus value produced with the trading and financial capitalists.

The notion of class is developed in terms of industrial and commercial capitalists set against industrial and commercial workers. The more the premises are modified by the addition of social parameters, the more refined our picture of class structure becomes. It is then clear that one's relation to the means of production is a decisive but not the sole characteristic for the definition of social classes. The class structure of a societal structure naturally includes not only basic classes defined by the existing mode of production (capitalists and wage labourers), but 'subsidiary' classes and social strata (peasants, petit bourgeoisie, intellectuals).

Therefore historical materialism, contrary to the objections of bourgeois scientists, does not deny the complex character of social class relations, but only refuses to allow the definitive class structure to be lost in a swamp of second-level indices and secondary relations.

Even though the further development of the model cannot be pursued here, the following can be: (a) the class concept obeys its own unique developmental logic which allows systematic refinement of its semantics; and (b) the existing theory can be modified and can grasp increasingly complex aspects of social reality by gradually increasing its own complexity. The level of the theory can be adapted to meet new demands for explanation.

As explanatory theory, the Marxist theory of class may be counted among the empircally nomothetic sciences. But its materialist approach, orientation to ideology-criticism and revolutionary solidarity, enable it to offer a theory and practice extending beyond this type.

There is a permanent structural link between classes and class struggle in regard to the form of a society: 'Social classes do not exist *a priori*, as such, in such a way that they eventually engage in class struggle, which would allow the assumption that there were classes without class conflict . . . The analysis of classes, which includes conflict between classes as well as political and ideological circumstances, describes the objective positions taken up by agents within the societal division of labour: these positions are independent of the will of those agents . . . This structural determination of classes, which here appear only in the form of class conflict, must nevertheless be distinguished from the position of classes in the economy, which is the place where the historical individuality of a societal formation, in short the actual situation of the class struggle, is concentrated.'[4] That affords the major components of a definition:

(a) Class conflict is the direct reflection of the original antagonism of the mode of production (between capital and labour) on the level of social conditions.

(b) Class struggle does not concern only the economic structure, but from the start the political and ideological sector. Political contradictions and ideological controversies are not to be confused with economic positions, but are, exactly like economic exploitation, objective aspects of class rule.

(c) The structural definition of class conflict therefore makes it impossible to reduce it to mere confrontations of economic interests and individual decisions.

(d) Individual fractions of social classes do not necessarily behave in accordance with their structural nature. A typical example of this is the 'worker aristocracy' in industrial concerns which is dependent on wages but co-operates politically and ideologically with the bourgeois class position.

(e) In this sense one can change class positions, but in general one cannot merely by one's individual decision withdraw altogether from the class struggle.

(f) Even a wholly ethically desirable solution to class conflict and a change of procedure in the class struggle remain illusionary as long as its causes are not removed.

Since class conflict has a polarized structure (that is, its components are mutually conditioned by opposition), it is essentially unstable; this gives rise to a dynamic process. This process occurs in one direction as forceful stablization of class division by the ruling class, and in another direction as the attempt of the oppressed class to end class division by eventually establishing a classless society. An ultimate end to class conflict can therefore only come about if progress is made to a higher form of society in which the causes of class division are removed.

THEORETICAL AND PRACTICAL ASPECTS OF THE CHALLENGE TO CATHOLIC SOCIAL TEACHING

Catholic social teaching, insofar as it claims to be a theological discipline, and appears in that form, must offer respectable solutions in the following problematic areas:

Catholic social teaching has to define its own scientific understanding and its position in theoretical scientific discourse. An important step in this direction would be a refinement of the logical form of its own propositions. Is Catholic social teaching really based on empirically substantial, analytically proven propositions regarding historical and social reality? Surely its premisses lay claim to descriptive content but are no more than normative judgments or wishful prescriptions (if not mere illusionary hypotheses) about reality. Catholic social teaching is far too often arrested at the stage of generalizations: commonplace assessments of phenomena that are only halfway to an explanation.

The questions I have asked not only demand a more scientifically responsible form of self-reflection, but a redefinition of contents. The form and method of data assembly also need rethinking. In this regard, the methodological relevance of political options also have to be rethought, and the basis of interest and practical orientation of Catholic social teaching require thorough investigation. Its frequent attempts to separate class conflict from the existence of classes put it into close theoretical and practical union with bourgeois social science, and are supported by capitalist organizations.

The theoretical level of the Marxist analysis of classes and class conflict forces Catholic social teaching to revise many of its suppositions about that theory, but above all to discard a journalistic and simplistic approach in regard to Marxism and to replace it with a form of meta-theoretical discourse conducted in accordance with testable rules. Notwithstanding objections to the contrary, Marxism is well acquainted with the distinction between truth and falsehood on the level of theory, but it examines a truth claim not in terms of a positivistic notion of the correspondence theory of truth, but in the context of a critical understanding of the relationship between theory and praxis.

Catholic social teaching must declare its own class standpoint, justify it, and if necessary revise it. That it does represent a class standpoint in theory and practice is especially clear from the following points—the initiators (conservative bishops and right-wing proponents of Catholic social teaching)[5] are almost always the same:

(a) A worldwide campaign is being conducted from Federal Germany against the theology of liberation; prominent members of the *Adveniat* organization are involved at an important level. In theory this is a hunt behind the screen of Catholic social teaching for latent Marxism in the thinking of many Latin American theologians. In fact an attempt is being made to split the Latin American Church.

(b) Anti-Communism is used as an emotional instrument by theoretical advisers to the magisterium and church organizations, and Catholic social teaching is cited as a justification for this, as if anti-Communism were an essential part of all that Jesus and his followers stand for. The position papers of the international organizations CAJ and MIJARC were fiercely attacked by ideological centres in the Federal Republic calling in question their alleged use of Marxist analysis.

(c) An entire series of volumes has been devoted to an attack on the political left in church organizations and is an attempt to justify the campaign theoretically. Church bodies also advise leading Catholic businessmen and openly advance reactionary social theories.[6]

The right-wing representatives of Catholic social teaching show by this conduct how they themselves wage class warfare, and organize themselves in that struggle as an anti-revolutionary force. The circles to which I refer not only openly contradict the obvious solidarity of the papal encyclicals with the working class, but are contrary to the political commitment of many progressive Christians all over the world.

Translated by J. Maxwell

Notes

1. Cf. A. Jasinska and L. Nowak, 'Grundlagen Marxschen Klassentheorie. Eine Rekonstruktion', in: J. Ritsert (ed.), *Zur Wissenschaftslogik einer kritischen Soziologie* (Frankfurt, 1976), pp. 175–213, esp. p. 179. I rely subsequently to a great extent on the results of this work.

2. See K. Marx to J. Weydemeyer, in Marx-Engels, *Werke*, vol. 28, pp. 507 ff.

3. See K. Marx, *Das Kapital*, vol. 1, Marx-Engels, *Werke*, vol. 23, pp. 590, 607, 669 f.

4. N. Poulantzas, *Klassen im Kapitalismus heute* (West Berlin, 1975), p. 14.

5. Cf. the colloquium of the study circle 'Church and Liberation' held from March 2 to 7 in Rome; among the participants were: Bishop Franz Hengsbach, Bishop Alfonso Lopez, Roger Vekemans, Anton Rauscher, Wilhelm Weber, E. Stehle. See the reports by KNA (no. 53 of 4 March 1976 and no. 54 of 5 March 1976).

6. Cf. especially the two series *Kirche und Gesellschaft,* published by the Centre for Catholic Social Studies in Mönchengladbach, and *Katholische Soziallehre in Text und Kommentar,* published by the Union of Catholic Entrepreneurs, the Catholic Employers Movement and the Kolpingwerk Deutscher Zentralverband.

Hans-Hermann Hücking

The Christian Life and Church
Institutions within the Socialist State

THE chief goal of the Church as a diplomatic body, as manifested, for example, in the Vatican's policy towards the Eastern bloc, is to ensure a state guarantee for the Church's power structure, the validity of canon law and the preservation at all costs of the practice of religion in the social system. This the socialist state can well afford to permit, for reasons of political opportunism, because its own sphere of jurisdiction is in no way endangered. In return, the Church ensures the political loyalty of both clergy and laity, though this is limited to the practical context of living and working together, and does not go as far as the profession of faith in the political-ideological doctrines of the socialist state. The decisive factor in the development of relations between church and state in eastern Europe since the 1960's has been the Vatican's recognition that the social system prevailing there can no longer be regarded as a temporary phenomenon to be overthrown as soon as possible. This point of view was firmly rooted in Rome at the very latest after the events in Hungary in 1956. The ratification of the *status quo* in Europe formulated in Helsinki in 1975 (KSZE), in which the Vatican played its part, has also been formally adopted by the churches in eastern Europe.

The mutual co-operation, though for different motives, between the socialist state and the Catholic Church not only threatens the existence of (informal) critical groups both within and on the fringe of the Church, but also excludes the Church's intervention on the part of the oppressed. 'Within the Communist power bloc writers and scientists and their families are running the risk of life-long incarceration in prisons, labour camps and lunatic asylums. But instead of confronting the ideology behind this system harshly but directly, Rome contents itself with generalized 'concepts of freedom' without any ideological commitment. The Church's strategy of salvation is based first and foremost on the actual individual who risks his own freedom and his own life in the struggle against violence and oppression, in order to achieve freedom for all.'[1]

There are considerable differences between state and church in the various socialist countries which must always be taken into consideration. But they do have a common identity of the same inner power structure.[2] This structure is primarily directed inwards in order to prevent the possibility of any potential or latent movements in the direction of democratic socialism or internal reform within the Church.

It should also be noted how the social function of the Church declines rapidly in socialist countries. The Church's power to integrate and form the consciousness of its members has only remained unchanged among older people and among those who either feel alienated by or reject the concept of social or economic development, or who have drifted completely away from it—in other words, the fringe groups. The criterion for identification with the institutional Church increases in porportion to the degree of distance from social life. Socio-economic changes have struck particularly harshly at the ordinary membership of the Church. At the intermediary level, the clergy was not forced to such a great extent to accept the implications of the new situation. The highest level of the church hierarchy, the episcopate, was able to evade the challenge presented by these changes. Individuals or groups of the laity who understand the Church to be 'the people of God on the path to salvation' find themselves confronted by an ecclesiology and bureaucratic organization in which involvement on the part of the ordinary member is either ignored or blocked. The Church's power structure and desire to serve its own interests ensure the maintenance of the *status quo*, the semblance of being a church of the people, traditional theology and the paternalistic church model.[3]

The phenomenon of small lay groups that have come into being in socialist countries in opposition to traditional ecclesiology and church institutions is to all intents and purposes ignored by church leaders or denounced as pro-western in tendency—and in this they concur with the official party line. These groups combine their demand for a new ecclesiology and a 'more democratic' church organization with a demand for the total overthrow of dogmatism and for the genuine democratization of all social structures. These groups, which are fundamentally non-dogmatic in outlook,[4] agree either partially or wholeheartedly with the aims of those Marxists accused of 'deviation to the right' by the Communist party.[5]

The opposition in socialist countries tends to be inherently systematized; however, the 'Christian wing' is distinguished by its essentially provisional character. The less publicity and organization these groups have at their disposal, the more effective they tend to be. They do not pursue any specific political or politico-religious aims; their chief concern is to effect a change of consciousness. Publicity disturbs the process of fermentation, alarms the hesitant, and alienates the 'conservatives'. They are frightened by the power of the church apparatus with its threats of existential sanctions. Owing to its traditional ecclesiology the church bureaucracy tends to give ideological as well as practical priority to institutional unity and regards anything that appears to question this unity as a threat to its very being.[6]

POLAND

Wiez

In February 1958 the monthly journal *Wiez* appeared for the first time in Warsaw. It was a manifestation of the more liberal tendencies that had come into the open as a result of the events of 'October '56'. In the same period the government permitted the establishment of five 'Clubs for Catholic Intellectuals' (KIK) in Warsaw, Craców, Wrocaw, Poznán and Torún. To this day they are the only groups of independent Catholics who have never made any secret of their critical solidarity with the episcopate and their pragmatically loyal attitude towards the government. Nevertheless in contrast to PAX and the Christian Socialist Society (CHSS) they have never at any time been supported by the government or the party (PZRP). At the very most, they have only been tolerated.[7] The Wiez circle is associated with the KIKs, and it has the same critical approach to Church and society as is expressed by the clubs.

The *Wiez* circle engages in a dialogue with non-believers and members of other faiths along the lines of a round-table discussion, in the conviction that Polish society must be based on a broadly-conceived pluralism, and that socialist structures must be continually developed and made more humane. But this presupposes acceptance of Poland's socio-economic foundation. 'One cannot fight for the humanistic perspectives of socialism if one remains mentally alienated from it.'[8]

By means of its publications—in addition to the journal it publishes the *Biblioteka Wiezi* which now has more than thirty titles on its list—*Wiez* is trying to ensure that this involvement does not stop at mere generalizations and declarations. The fundamental problems of Polish society, to which both Marxists and Catholics must seek a solution, including school reform, more humane living conditions, the role of women, sexuality, mental health, social policies, etc., are frequently discussed.

In addition to this, *Wiez* is fighting for a 'more open Catholicism'. 'We want "the other side" to acknowledge the cultural rôle of Polish Catholicism. We want non-believers in Poland to regard Christianity not as an irrelevant relic of the past, but as a vital force in contemporary culture' (Editor-in-Chief Mazowiecki). In the past the relationship between *Wiez* and the Church has been anything but peaceful. For example, a couple of years ago Cardinal Wyszyński forbade the clergy to publish anything in the journal because a group of Dominicans had published an article criticizing certain aspects of the Church. Even now, any member of the clergy who wishes to contribute an article to *Wiez* must first obtain formal permission from his bishop.

In the spring of 1968 Mazowiecki proposed a parliamentary enquiry in favour of students and intellectuals protesting against censorship and cultural oppression. To the 'New Left' this was the expression of a politically independent way of thinking.[9] The New Left consists of Marxists who are critical of the power structures of both Party and government and who deplore the way Marxist theory has been distorted into a closed system of thought.[10] Especially in the Warsaw KIK a fairly intensive dialogue has been carried on since 1968 between the New Left and the Catholics of the *Wiez* circle. The club became a meeting place for those Christians and Marxists who are concerned about cultural, scientific and religious freedom in Poland.

In March 1975 the committee of the Warsaw KIK issued a directive to its young members to suspend all contact with representatives of the New Left for three months in the first instance. The leaders of the club had obviously received a warning from the party that this 'subversive' association between critical Catholics and 'revisionist' Marxists could no longer be tolerated.

'Groups of the Common Path'

Informal Christian groups have existed in Poland since the end of the sixties, although to date there has been no discussion with or about them, let alone coverage in the Catholic press. A particular characteristic of these so-called 'Groups of the Common Path' (GW) is their demand that more attention be paid to the subject of human rights within the Church.

During the Council the pastoral office of the diocese of Katowice asked the lecturer in ecclesiastical history at the local seminary, Dr Gustaw Klapuch, to hold lectures on religious topics, followed by discussion, for intellectuals in the cities of Upper Silesia. These gatherings were often attended by thousands, and spontaneously led to the establishment of open discussion evenings on topics chosen by the participants. The laity themselves were responsible for organizing these evenings, and in this way the 'Groups of the Common Path' were formed on an informal basis. Priests were forbidden by their bishops to take part; outspoken groups of priests in the movement had to give up their meetings under pressure from the Curia. In a combined memorandum to the Bishop of Katowice in November 1969 the groups demanded that more attention be paid to the theme of human rights within the Church than is the case in a non-ecclesiastical community.

In 1970 Dr Klapuch was faced with the choice of dropping his demands for more human rights within the Church, giving up his work with the priests' groups and revising the structure of the meetings with the laity, or alternatively accepting his dismissal from his teaching post at the seminary as well as from the theological academy in Warsaw. On the pretext of 'anti-Catholic activities' Klapuch was suspended from his teaching post in the summer of 1970 and deported to Upper Silesia as assistant to the parish priest in the town of Tarnowskie Gory which has a population of 800.[11] Within a matter of weeks virtually all church rooms were barred to the groups. So from then on they met in private homes. But since meetings in private homes are seen as politically suspect in Poland, the groups found themselves once more forced to define their religious status within the Church.

Both discussion and social practice of the groups is concentrated on the polarity between the Old and New Testament and human rights. Questions about Christian practice are discussed at their monthly meetings, though the confrontation with church traditions and demands for reform are approached more cautiously. After lengthy internal consultations they eventually made a public statement defining their position on such themes as: the relation between religion and politics; between Church and justice in the world; between Church and state; informal groups in the Church; more 'democracy' in the Church; and the practice of confession and the celebration of the liturgy. Communication is maintained between the different groups, of which there are now about forty, numbering a total membership of approximately one thousand, not only by personal contact but also by exchanging detailed accounts of their respective meetings. Since the summer of 1974 a small hectographed magazine (*Nasza droga*—'Our Path') has been appearing at irregular intervals with a circulation of about 1500 copies. There is no intention of setting up a more tautly organized structure. As far as possible the groups should maintain their informal and independent character. However this aim encountered further difficulties in 1975–76. In the diocese of Katowice increasing attempts are being made to integrate these groups into the parishes and to place them under the watchful eye of the clergy. Informal groups are still being verbally approved by the Curia, but they are only given church recognition if they submit to church control.

Although most of the members of these groups are practising Catholics they have for some time now increasingly been accused of disloyalty to the Church. In a sermon held in the diocese of Katowice on 12.10.1975 they were described as 'pseudo-apostolic groups claiming to be Catholic, but in reality involved in political activities and not in agreement with the hierarchy'. The context of this statement makes it clear that it is referring not only to PAX or the CHSS but to the 'Groups of the Common Path' or GW. Though the latter have no connection with the political aspirations of PAX or the CHSS, it is obvious that they are not considered to be in 'agreement with the hierarchy' and hence denied any recognition as an official church group by the episcopacy.

For these groups the concept of human rights has for a long time symbolized their own understanding of humanity. The awareness that their own Church is failing to find a solution to the problems of human rights must inevitably lead to inner conflict and to a crisis of identity with their parish community. As yet there is no concrete evidence of the attitude of the state bureaucracy to the theories and practices of the GW groups. In any event, their demand for human rights (even if 'only' within the Church) will in the long run have its effect on the social process as a whole.

THE GERMAN DEMOCRATIC REPUBLIC

New appointments and changes in the hierarchy of the Church in the German Democratic Republic (in 1970–71 there were changes in the top ranks of five of the seven dioceses) coincided with the removal from office or dismissal of those who held views contrary to the official position of the Church.[12] The choice of new bishops appointed was indicative of a specific political tendency; namely, the increasingly centralized and powerful primacy of Cardinal Bengsch of Berlin. The dominance of the bishop of the Berlin diocese is of vital consquence for the overall situation of the Church in the German Democratic Republic. Firstly, it leads to the avoidance wherever possible of anything that might result in additional state intervention and to the curtailment within the Church of certain pastoral activities; secondly, the intensification of the central power structure as a protection against any new developments among the laity which might be difficult to control.

With reference to the first of these points, 'suitable pastoral ministry' is taken to mean parish work including church services, parish groups and charitable work in the approved traditional context. All efforts should be concentrated on maintaining the current standing of parish communities and the Church's field of activity. The central issue is to keep things as they are. Everything that can be seen to serve this end is upheld. But anything that clearly does not is cut back. Whenever the limits of straightforward pastoral care were exceeded those responsible were removed from their posts. This applied in particular to those dealing with children and students. With reference to the second point mentioned above, a Church which is so concerned with its own standing has no interest in 'looking outwards'. in participating in a dialogue with those who do not hold its beliefs. There is no dialogue between hierarchy and laity. 'The laity do not participate in the mission of the Church, though this is a right which cannot be denied.'[13] Any priest who does not see eye to eye with his bishop only has two alternatives. He can either strive for unity at any price, or he can give up his service to the Church and hence renounce the very basis of his existence.[14] A Church which permits internal debate, is outward-looking, can encompass a variety of different opinions and includes the laity in this process would not be sufficiently manoeuvrable given the prevailing political circumstances. It would be too vulnerable to influence from outside the Church and would thus endanger itself unnecessarily (Bengsch). Such an outlook is based on a specific idea that the Church determined by : separation from the outside world, the formulation of policy only within the narrow confines of the hierarchy, a strict order of authority emanating from the hierarchy to the ranks below, and the limitation of lay participation to church services and charitable work, all of which corresponds to the expectations of the state.[15]

Not all Catholics in the German Democratic Republic are in agreement with this, as has been amply proved by the 'letter circle' organized by Fr Karl Herbst since 1958. In 1970 he had about 1700 subscribers of which just about half were Catholic priests. The 'letter circle' aimed, by means of personal contact and the letters edited by Herbst tolerated and even with the approval of the church leaders), to promote greater mutual understanding between the clergy of both churches and to inform them of current theological debates in Catholic circles throughout the world. However, when it became apparent that the policies being pursued by Rome were leading to ecumenical stagnation and the reassertion of a more rigid approach, and that this was being strongly supported by the bishops of the GDR, conflict between the 'letter circle' and the official Church was inevitable. Herbst saw no alternative but to resign[16], and since 1971 he has been working as an orderly in a state hospital. In 1975 the letter service came to an end after the confiscation of the copying machine by the state authorities. As Herbst did not have a licence to use it, he paid a fine of 500 Marks.

Between 1964 and 1969 a group from Halle tried by means of open letters to establish a public debate on the question of social involvement of Christians in the GDR. Although they made their 'Correspondence' (about two hundred copies) available to the bishops, student groups and those priests and members of the laity who expressed interest, there was never any official reaction from the hierarchy. The bishops did, however, make their attitude known by means of deliberately indiscreet comments. So long as these comments contented themselves with references to 'psychopaths' and people lifting ideas from western journals, the group was only superficially affected. But when it was rumoured from professorial circles that this group was undoubtedly operating on orders received from the Ministry for State Security, an atmosphere of mistrust was created which had a crippling effect on their work. This was followed up by official church statements that the critical attitude towards society expressed in the 'Correspondence' was damaging to the good relationship that was beginning to develop between the Church and the state. The group thus made the painful discovery that any initiative to establish a free exchange of ideas within the Church was blocked by such insidious statements and forced into a precarious isolation. A third example of the fate of radical Christian groups in the GDR is provided by the 'Halle Action Group' (AKH). Founded in 1969, this group consisted of about an hundred engaged Christians, of which the majority were members of the clergy. In their 'provisional declaration of intent' of 1969 they advocated a more democratic and humane approach as being the chief aim of church renewal. At present, the Church in the GDR in effect supported the state by means of its authoritarian structures and attitudes. The traditional power structures of both Church and state were 'so similiar, that although basically diametrically opposed, they in effect confirm and support each other'.[17] Since 1969 the Halle Action Group has published signed type-written articles stating their attitude to matters of social and religious concern. However, it has not as yet been recognized by the bishops as a 'legitimate church organization with pastoral aims'.[18]

The Halle Action Group is critical of 'radical socialism' but not of the kind of socialism that includes and promotes the freedom and rights of its citizens. It is this reservation which principally alienates the group from the aims of the Christian Democratic Union in the GDR and the 'Berlin Conference of Catholic Christians from the European States'.[19] The Halle group is concerned first and foremost with 'fundamental democracy' in the institutions of the Church and with the increase of shared responsibility and participation of all who wish to identify themselves, even if only partially, with the Church.

Despite the occasional latent or explicit conflict between the church administration and socialist bureaucracy in the countries of Eastern Europe, both these bodies share similar interests and are in mutual agreement as to the necessity of resisting any radical activities or alternative proposals on the part of those whom they have in their care or govern.

The Christians in question were nearly all born after the war. They see the promotion of socialism as a challenge and though critical in some respects, they seek a positive response to it. In embracing 'radical socialism' they also accept the practical conditions this presupposes and some of the ideological implications involved. Theirs is not a blind, unequivocal affirmation, but rather a conscious recognition of a complicated process which began in difficult historical circumstances. These Christians are also attempting to find theological affirmation of the basic principles of Marxist theory and to interpret social problems, in particular those in their own countries, in accordance with the tenets of historical materialism. In doing this, they are laying themselves open to the suspicion of opportunism and revisionism, and hence find themselves under pressure from both church and state authorities. The leaders of the Church see them as disrupting relations with the state and causing dissension within the Church, and even cast doubt on their Christianity. Nor do they fit into the old schema of the Marxist-Leninist criticism of religion. The party functionaries find it incomprehensible that the Christian faith can apparently sever its old ideological commitments and join forces with declared Marxists, even if these are at times discredited as dissidents.

These Christians are still branded as fringe groups. They are forced to undergo the painful experience of seeing their faith, their approach to Christian existence and their legitimacy questioned by the church hierarchy. They have to defend themselves in the most difficult circumstances. By their very existence they cast doubt on the Christian legitimacy of the prevailing outlook of the official Church in the socialist countries.

Translated by Sarah Twohig

Notes

1. Statement issued by the Paulus-Gesellschaft on the current Vatican policy towards Eastern Europe on 19 February 1974.
2. 'Any group [of Christians] which contravenes the control of the Church is

no longer under the control of the state'—the testified statement of a leading official of the State Security Service of the GDR in 1969.

3. Miklós Tomka, 'The Changing Role of Church Institutions in Hungary' (unpublished manuscript).

4. The concept 'non-dogmatic' applies to any form of criticism and opposition in Eastern European countries which consciously or unconsciously acknowledges the basic socialist principles of the system or the prevailing ideology. It also applies to any unarticulated, anti-dictatorial protest among the population so long as this is not caused by explicitly anti-Communist or conservative motives rejecting socialism in any form.

5. As, e.g., the group around András Hegedüs and Ágnes Heller denounced as 'right-wing and revisionist' by the Hungarian Labour Party: cf. *Frankfurter Hefte*, 8/1974, pp. 547 ff.

6. Stephan H. Pfürtner, 'Die Menschenrechte in der römisch-katholischen Kirche', in *Zeitschrift für evangelische Ethik,* 20/1 (Gütersloh, 1976), p. 48f.

7. Cf. Józefa Hennelowa, 'Die ''Znak-Bewegung'' ', in: *Pax-Christi-info*, 9/5–6, 1974, pp. 11ff.

8. Quoted by Tadeusz M. Swiecicki, 'Was Staat und Kirche fürchten', in Publik-Forum, 5/1976, pp. 20f.

9. Andrzej Peliński, 'Poland: Was denkt die Opposition', in: *Publik-Forum*, 9/1974, p. 9.

10. One document published by this neo-Marxist opposition group is the 'Open Letter to the Party' by Jacek Kuroń and Karol Modzelewski.

11. Klapuch was given a partial pardon after the Synod of Bishops held in Rome in October 1974 when he was offered a lectureship in church history at the 'Institute for the Laity' in Katowice.

12. These included the student pastor Theo Mechtenberg (Magdeburg), the former student pastor in Halle and later parish priest in Merseburg, Adolf Brockhoff, as well as Father Karl Herbst.

13. According to the Leipzig Oratorian Wolfgang Trilling, 1967.

14. Clemens Rosner (Leipzig), in *SOG-Papiere*, 1/1970, p. 14 f.

15. 'Because the government of the GDR, in accordance with the findings of socialist sociologists, practises a ''democratic centralism'' in which the rights of the individual are in effect subordinate to the dictates of society, it therefore expects a similar hierarchical order within the Church.' J. Huhn, 'Die Existenz der Christen im Sozialismus, insbesondere in der DDR', in *Internationale Dialog-Zeitschrift,* vol. 4 (Freiburg-im-Breisgau, 1974), p. 344.

16. 'No ordinary in the GDR may permit the letter service . . . as an organ for free discussion and spread of information. The transfer to a parish instead of the pastoral work in Rötha should . . . make it impossible to continue this work. But I cannot give up the letter service . . . since November last year 1240 readers have explicitly requested that it continue, and because free information and open discussion is also necessary in our church circles.' *SOG-Papiere*, p. 198.

17. Quoted in KNA-Information Service, no. 25 (22.6) 1975, p. 7.

18. In May 1976 Bishop Johannes Braun, the Apostolic Administrator of Magdeburg, rejected an application for permission to use a church-owned

youth hostel for a family weekend of the Halle Action Group on the grounds that the group was 'not a recognized church association, and therefore was not entitled to use one of our houses'.

19. The Bishops' Conference regards the Church more as an instrument which can assist in realizing the political aims of the SED and CDU. In the same way the Halle Action Group regards itself as a group within the Church whose solidarity should 'under no circumstances' lead to 'disagreement with the bishop' which can 'be manipulated from outside by certain parties'. Clemens Rosner, *op. cit.*, p. 15.

Hansjakob Stehle

Christianity and Socialism:
Some Aspects of State Policy
towards Religion and Church Policy

A MODUS VIVENDI

ATHEISM has now become an inseparable part of the ideology of the state in all countries in which the Communist party has a monopoly of power. In all these countries, a genuine dialogue between Christians and socialists has been blocked because the problem is only to a very limited extent (or not at all) regarded as a theological or ideological one, but above all as a question of practical politics in a specific historical context. In other words, every reflection about the 'essence' of the Church, in an attempt to do away with anything that is not part of that essence in a spirit of reform, and any search for a theology that is orientated towards the future which might result from an examination of points of contact between a socialist orientation towards the future in this world and a Christian orientation towards the hereafter is made meaningless, as long as the question is restricted on both sides to the quest for a *modus vivendi*. This applies whether the latter is regarded as possibly peaceful survival of religion or whether it is seen as a painless dying away of religion. Both the communist policy towards religion and the Catholic Ostpolitik have moved between these two aims since 1917.

Lenin's 'separation of Church and state', decreed in January 1918 was not based, as in western models, on the state's agnostic and neutral attitude towards religion. This 'separation' stripped the Church of its privileges and even its legal personality (art. 12). It reduced freedom of

religion to a simple freedom to worship and even made the latter subject to control by the state, a system which remained basically the same
from its first drafting (23 January 1929) to its most recent modification
(3 July 1975).[1] The 'separation' therefore has retained a distinctly dis-
criminatory character. Its aim was, of course, to combat the spread of
the 'religious fog' which was, in Lenin's view, an instrument used by
the exploiting class and, when that class had disappeared, a 'residue' of
its power. According to this way of thinking, religion is socially harmful
because it is socially, socio-psychologically and class-conditioned. It is
therefore a phenomenon towards which the state cannot be indifferent.

It is true to say that the Soviet state was obliged, for reasons of state
and because of political opportunism and tactics, to modify this to-
talitarian attitude towards religion. This modification was also necessary because what is so obviously true after almost sixty years of
Soviet socialism became apparent very soon, namely that religion
was—contrary to all the Marxist-Leninist forecasts of an early
death—quite capable of surviving independently of any fixed pattern of
society. Neither Lenin nor Stalin and his successors, however, were
tempted to take such a utopian measure as that taken in Albania in
1967. The Albanian leader, Enver Hoxha, officially dissolved all religious communities at that time and had their places of worship destroyed. He then declared that Albania was the 'first atheistic state in
the world'.

The churches in Albania (and probably also in China), then, can now
only have an underground way of life, an existence in the catacombs.
We are bound to ask in this context whether this is preferable to a legal
minimum existence that is controlled and discriminated against by the
state. This was the question that confronted the Russian Orthodox and
the small Russian Catholic churches after the October revolution. Pa-
triarch Tikhon, whose courage has often been contrasted with the
adaptability of his successors, at first took up a very uncompromising
position. Without any sign of fear of the possible consequences for
himself, he described Lenin's decree on religion as the 'work of the
devil'. As soon as he realized, however, that the external structure of
his Church was threatened with total destruction if the minimum existence offered by the state was rejected, he set out to achieve an agreement with the Soviet government, without at the same time losing the
trust of the members of his Church.

THE NEED FOR AGREEMENT

The Catholic Church was also confronted by this question and re-
sponded in a similar way. The secretary of state Cardinal Gasparri, an

experienced papal diplomat, insisted that the 'blood of the martyrs has always been the best seed of the Church', yet for years negotiated with the Soviet government, in the service of Benedict XV and Pius XI, so that the Catholics of Russia would be spared martyrdom.[2]

The Vatican has for a long time been prepared to make concessions, to such an extent that, in 1927, Moscow's 'political objections' to the bishops' candidates were taken seriously enough for only 'priests acceptable to the government' to be sent to Russia. It was not until twenty years after the revolution, when Stalin's reign of terror put an end to 'hope against hope', that the pope condemned the Soviet system for the first time (*Divini Redemptoris*, 1937).

These historical experiences continued to have an effect when towards the end of the nineteen-fifties, after the death of Stalin, the Vatican began to tie up loose ends in the relationship. This was all the more important to do, because so many states had, since 1945, become socialist on the Soviet pattern, many of them, such as Poland, Hungary and Czechoslovakia, with large Catholic populations. The Vatican therefore also attempted to establish the extent to which the policies of the other Communist countries, with their various national and religious traditions, were different from the Russian model.

THE POLICY OF *DO UT DES*

In 1972, Mgr Agostino Casaroli, the Vatican adviser for public affairs, looking back over a period of years, declared that two contrasting but related factors had played a part in the hostile policy of the Eastern European Communist states towards religion. On the one hand, anti-religious reasons had been concealed behind ostensibly 'political' motives. On the other hand, however, the Marxist leaders had accepted these anti-religious reasons as political.[3] There are two reasons for this, according to Casaroli. The first is that these Communist leaders had always thought of religion simply and solely as a political phenomenon. In the second place, 'the Church is not simply the bearer of a spiritual and eschatological message; it also acts with authority in providing moral guide-lines for Christian activity in the personal and public spheres'.

The Communist governments would perhaps have been strongly motivated to seek agreement with the Vatican if the Catholic Church had recognized 'the socialist ordering of society as an inviolable and patriotically orientated reality'. This was stated by the Polish minister for Church affairs, Skarżyński, on 10 October 1971. In this statement, he was certainly expressing a view similar to that of the Soviet leaders, who had not been prepared until then to deal with the Vatican in questions relating to the Church itself, but had a powerful reason for making the Catholic Church politically neutral, especially in Poland. They might also have been ready to pay a certain price for this. It is, however, very doubtful whether Skarzyński was acting in accordance with the Soviet intention when he said: 'The people's state will respect the lasting character of the religious activity of the Church and appreciate the social value of its educational function with regard to believers'.[4] Indeed, this statement was a blow at the roots of Leninist state atheism and no other representative of an Eastern European state has, to my knowledge, gone as far as this. This statement possibly laid the foundations for a long-term *do ut des* diplomacy, in which the pragmatic aim of safeguarding power might be more important than ideological orthodoxy.

STRUCTURAL CONDITIONS FOR THE SURVIVAL OF THE CHURCH

Does this mean that the Church's continued existence will be guaranteed provided that it once again becomes a factor providing stability in the existing social order, in this case a socialist order? Is its function to be that of neo-integralism in a new political context or simply that of 'political asceticism'? Is it to demonstrate neutrality, loyalty at a distance and a pure love of one's enemy? These questions are taken very seriously by the Roman Curia and a great deal of thought has been given to them in recent years, although little of this has reached the public. In the view of the Vatican, the problem has resolved itself into three groups of questions:

1. What has to be guaranteed diplomatically? Is it more important to act pastorally or to resist politically? (The latter is often inseparable from national resistance.) Is it possible to separate the two?

2. Are hierarchical structures indispensable if pastoral work is effectively to be carried out? Or does the Spirit blow where it will even when the Church structures are weak or even absent?

3. Should a 'pastoral policy' towards socialist countries only serve the interests of the Church or should it also serve those of religious freedom 'as such', toleration, peace (between men and states) and social and national liberation?

The Vatican answer to these questions follows certain theological guide-lines, which can be summarized as follows.[5] In the first place, *salus animarum suprema lex*. The salvation of individual souls as the supreme commandment is defined, in the post-conciliar (as in the pre-conciliar) Church, eschatologically; in other words, it transcends history. The Church is therefore not subject to any political or social system. It stands up for man's basic rights in all systems and especially for the right of religious freedom, because it is a 'sign of man's personal transcendence'.

The Church can only carry out its saving mission as a 'visible assembly' or a 'society formed and ordered in this world'. Only priests, who have been given full powers, can—with the exception of emergency baptism—administer the sacraments that are necessary for salvation. The continuity of the priesthood is guaranteed only within the hierarchical structure, which is supported by the bishops. The appointment of bishops is therefore, according to Casaroli, essential for the long-term survival of the Church.

Viewed from outside the Catholic understanding of the Church, this type of argument is, of course, questionable. Evangelical or free churches, for which such 'structures' are not essential, can survive within a framework of state atheism without any relationship with the established powers. They are also exposed to attack and seizure insofar as their existence can be seized.

Pressure on the Catholic and Orthodox churches has, however, given rise to a certain nostalgia for the early Church among members of those churches living in the diaspora and this has often led, unconsciously to a 'reformed' concept of the Church. This and similar tendencies, which are, again often unconsciously, orientated towards ideas of the Church that are based on religious models of socialist communities, should not, in my opinion, be regarded as too important. All that we know about the situation points, after all, to the fact that the 'success' or 'failure' of attempts made by the Church to find a *modus vivendi* with the state have only been seriously criticized by those believers who think in purely political categories, in other words, who regard the Church as an organ of resistance to or collaboration with the state.

As far as the purely religious life of these and other Christians is concerned, the most important aspect is whether it is still possible to strengthen that life sacramentally and liturgically. According to Catholic teaching, this function can only be carried out by a priest, who may be subjectively unworthy, but who has been validly ordained. This may be a stumbling-block in the contemporary debate, but in the borderline situation into which religious life has been driven, in so many places, by state atheism it has become an objective fact of importance, even for non-believers. This is in itself evidence of the fact that religion, which was described by Marx as the ''sigh of the oppressed creature', is a much more basic need than many atheistic ideologists—and many theologians—suspect.

Translated by David Smith

Notes

1. Texts of the decrees of 1918 and 1929 will be found in N. Struve, *Die Christen in der UdSSR (Les Chrétiens en U.R.S.S)* (Mainz and Paris, 1965), pp. 461–76. The text of the Modifications of 1975 will be found in *Vedomosti Verkhovnogo Soveta RSFR*, no. 27 (873), pp. 487–91. See also G. Barberini, *Stati socialisti e confessioni religiose* (Milan, 1973).

2. See H. Stehle, *Die Ostpolitik des Vatikans, 1917–1975* (Munich, 1975), pp. 16 ff.

3. This and all the other quotations in my article are taken from Casaroli's address in Milan on 20 January 1972 *(Civiltà Cattolica*, no. 2920, 1972, and *Relazioni Internazionale,* no. 7, 1972). See also Casaroli's interview in *Die Presse* (Vienna) on 21 and 22 December 1974.

4. See Skarzyński's speech in *Slowo Powszechne* (Warsaw), 4 October 1971. In a quotation from this speech by I. Krasicki (*Argumenty*, Warsaw, 23 April 1972), the words 'lasting character' were left out.

5. This summary is based on the Dogmatic Constitution *Lumen gentium*, I 8, II 9, IV 28; the *Pastoral Constitution on the Church and the World*, IV 40. See also Casaroli's interview in *Die Presse*, *op. cit.*, and Mgr Giovanni Benelli's address in Vienna on 4 May 1976 (see *Documentation Catholique*, no. 1677, 6 June 1976).

Iring Fetscher

State Socialist Ideology as Religion?

THE doctrine of Marxism-Leninism became a compulsory state ideology under Stalin. In a phenomenological perspective, it has many features similar to those proper to a Church. The festive processions with portraits of the 'classical theorists' Marx, Engels, Lenin and—until 1956—Stalin, the replacement of the icon corner with a 'red corner', the rôle of the Central Committee as a College of Cardinals, the Party Days as Councils, the General Secretary and 'great leader' as a sort of Pope, even the double rôle of the head of state of the Soviet Union and the supreme head of the all-embracing union of Communist Parties: all that can be appropriately summarized under the heading 'church', 'secular church', or 'militant and orthodox Communist community of faith'. Even in the language of Communist cadres and disciples of Marxism-Leninism the analogy finds support. For instance, it is said that theory must be kept 'pure'. That would never be said of a scientific theory, which is properly developed, and always subject to new tests and so on, but never preserved in a pure form. The treatment of 'deviants' corresponds to the persecution of heretics in the Church as it was. Of course this phenomenological finding rather contradicts the way in which Marxist-Leninists see themselves. But even in their most emphatic statements about the non-tenability of religion, and in their energetic claims for the scientific nature of their own doctrine, the tone of the faithful is undeniable: 'The teaching of Marx is all-powerful because it is right. It is self-enclosed and harmonious; it offers a unified understanding of the world, which is irreconcilable with any form of superstitition or reaction' (Lenin). The claim to scientific status does not remove the religious characteristics of Marxism-Leninism as a state ideology. Instead its 'scientific nature' is shown to be an illusion. That was most obviously the case in the period of the 'personality cult' when Stalin alone could decide whether a certain theory of language, a natural scientific theorem, was 'Marxist' and therefore scientific or not. Leszek Kolakowski has called this kind of Marxism 'institutional Marxism' in order to distinguish it from intellectual Marxism, which is identical with the theories developed by Marx that to a considerable extent now form part of the content of the critical social sciences. But institutional Marxism is not a science but a doctrine. It cannot (or could not) be defined by specific methods or contents, but only be reference to an authority charged with its actual characterization. In Stalin's time that authority was the General Secretary of the Party, and since 1956 the function has to all intents and purposes been assumed by the collective leadership. The monarchical Church has become conciliar. 'The word ''Marxism'' ' writes Kolakowski,' never meant a doctrine defined by its content, but a doctrine which was decided quite formally and by the decree of an infallible institution, which in a certain period of world history was embodied in the 'greatest linguist', the 'greatest historian' the greatest philosopher' and 'greatest economic expert' in the world. In other words, the term 'Marxism' became a concept with an institutional and no intellectual content—as usually happens with any ecclesiastical decree.'[1]

Therefore we can define as a Marxist anyone who is ready 'to accept ideas which have been confirmed by authority', who in other words does not make any independent critical assessment of theses which he accepts as contents of faith. Kolakowski ironically describes the consequences of this attitude; 'For this very reason—in regard to the institutional and not intellectual nature of Marxism—the genuine Marxist acknowledges views the content of which he never needs to understand. As every Marxist knew in 1950, Lysenko's theory of heredity was correct, Hegel's philosophy was an aristocratic reaction to the French Revolution, Dostoevsky was a decadent, Babayevsky a first-class writer, Suvorov a vehicle of progress and the resonance theory in chemistry out-of-date nonsense. Every Marxist knew that was the case, even if he had heard nothing of chromosomes, did not know in what century Hegel lived, had never read even a story by Dostoevsky, and had never even worked through a lower secondary chemistry text-book. There was no need to concern himself with all that, for the content of Marxism was confirmed by authority'.[2]

This ironic description of Stalin's rôle in the determination of the 'valid' and 'binding' content of Marxism-Leninism recalls the confrontation of the Catholic Church with certain teachings of the modern natural sciences in the nineteenth century. In both cases the 'Churches' had to surrender, because the natural sciences had on their side the greater degree of evidence, and above all social utility. Even in the USSR modern genetics has been recognized in the meantime, the resonance theory in chemistry has been taken seriously, and even the long resisted relativity theory of Einstein has been accepted. The natural scientists have used their economic necessity to obtain space in which to work untrammelled by party and state tutelage.

Communist and socialist parties which are not themselves in power and which have to ground their policies on realistic analyses and win votes by convincing arguments have in recent years (especially since 1968) emancipated themselves from any form of censorship by a central court of judgment similar to that which operates in a church. The Italian Communists seek to establish a doctrinally neutral state (in the tradition of bourgeois liberalism and democracy) and understand Marxism as a method which has continually to be improved and corrected on the basis of experience, and not as dogma.

For critical Marxists who live in the Warsaw Pact and similar countries, however, or who are members of parties which still practise the dogmatic determination of the 'actual content' of the doctrine, conditions are different. Even when doctrine is generally restricted to historical and social reality (the dialectics of nature generally plays less of a part than in Stalin's time, even though it has not been dispensed with), there are still many restrictions on scientific work.

The critical application of Marxism suffers enormous difficulties in these countries; perhaps the worst is the simultaneous function of Marxism-Leninism as a state religion. One academic writing from such a country says: ' In our societies Marxism has a dual rôle: a religious and a cognitive. When the first is dominant the second is systematically repressed. Marxism cannot freely develop its cognitive possibilities. That may appear paradoxical, but it is the case. In countries where Marxism is the state ideology, Marxism appears to be the least developed cognitive theory. The system works against it. But perhaps Marxism includes a possible theory of our state socialist societies'. Under the conditions of compulsory faith subject to no critical checks, Marxism has clearly declined. It has lost credibility. It is on all lips but in no one's head. 'No one believes in it; the rulers don't, because they use it only for religious purposes; the ruled don't, because they hate it. The system works against Marxism. Perhaps the system is afraid of Marxism. . .'[3] Here Marxism which has become doctrine is no longer functioning as ideology, but has actually become an example of what the early French Enlightenment called priestly deception. A political élite which itself does not believe in the truth of its doctrine uses it as a means to legitimate its rule. If this function is to be retained, then no one 'outside the party' and outside the framework decided by the party leadership may engage in Marxist studies. Critical Marxism, which is capable of submitting its own social order to relentless scrutiny, becomes the most dangerous enemy. The calcification of theory for the purposes of legitimation stands in the way of its use as a means of analysis and orientation. The political leadership deprives itself of a valuable political instrument. They can influence no one outside, where populations are not subject to them, with this denatured, dogmatized and formalized ideology. A partial self-criticism and reformation is therefore not to be excluded, above all if undogmatic and critical Marxists are successful outside the Soviet orbit. Of course there is a tendency among the leaders of the eastern European states to compensate the lost of credibility of their state ideologies by improving the supply of consumer goods and invoking nationalism, the same means which 'bourgeois régimes' tend to use. If that policy succeeds, there could be a reduction in the religious rôle of the state ideology, but it is hardly conceivable that it will completely disappear, since it is the only means of legitimation of the political élite of the party leadership, who are engaged in a competitive struggle with the 'technocrats', the managers of the economy, for whom the state religion is superfluous.

If we accept that men have a fundamental need for meaningful fulfilment beyond the mere satisfaction of material needs, and that they look to ends which transcend individual existence, then it is not surprising that the eastern bloc countries feature a number of religious and pseudo-religious movements. Since the formally preserved state religions of Marxism-Leninism have increasingly lost credibility and attractiveness, and the lack of faith among many of the leaders is more or less obvious, this essential need strives more and more for ways to express itself. In an early martial phase revolutionary Marxism is certainly able to satisfy that genuine human need for meaningful existential satisfaction, but the same can no longer be true of a now sterile state doctrine, acknowledgment of which has become a presupposition of individual advancement in the bureaucracy. Critical Marxists who treat the theory with intellectual seriousness feel that they are minorities and outsiders in these states. They criticize both their own bureaucratic élites and those of the 'West' and those sections of their own population who are fascinated by the western way of life.

A critical description of the Church offered by Fichte more than 160 years ago can also serve as a description of the bureaucratic Church that the state party of the eastern states has become, and by and large corresponds to the critique made of that 'Church' by critical Marxists: 'If the Church [the state party] accepted its members' confessions of faith as mere hypocrisy, then its purpose would be destroyed; a confession of faith which is held to be false, cannot strengthen us in our faith. . . . The essential premiss without which no church constitution [no obligatory state ideology] is possible, is that its basic confession of faith contains without any doubt *the sole and pure truth* at which anyone in search of truth must arrive [insofar as he is instructed by the Church or the state party]; the second premiss is derived directly from the first: it is in the power of every man to evoke this conviction in himself if he wants to; lack of faith is always due either to a lack of attentive spirit or to stubbornness, and faith is dependent on our free will. Therefore all ecclesiastical systems [all state socialist ideocracies] make faith incumbent upon their members'.[4]

The basis of the Church as defined by Fichte does not apply to Marxism in its original form and in a pre-revolutionary society. There it is taken for granted that the members of the privileged classes (the industrial capitalists, the landowners, and so on) are always for the most part unable to perceive the truth of Marxism because that would prove an obstacle to their (unconsciously effective) interests. But this assumption no longer applies with the removal of private ownership of the means of production (or so Marxists hold), and henceforth there can be only two reasons for any lack of readiness to accept the state socialist 'faith': inadequate information ('instruction', training), or ill will. In view of the massive amount of indoctrination offered to the population from children's books to university, ill will is usually the diagnosis. At best the 'error' is assessed as only 'objectively' supporting the interests of the opponents of the régime, but deviant opinions are also often interpreted as decisive opposition. On the other hand, readiness to accept the canon of binding truths (modifiable in content by the party) is taken as evidence of readiness for unquestioning obedience. It is only this obedience that is impostant; the leaders are less and less concerned with the *content* of the doctrine. What Karl Korsch called the 'decline of the great method' (Brecht's term for Marxism) is intimately linked to this change of function.

The Christian Church has nothing to fear from the critical aspect of a Marxist doctrine which has become a state ideology. Here the dangers are to be found only in the region of administrative pressure—a pressure which is also put on the 'supporters' of the particular belief system and thus renders the faith itself unacceptable. Where acceptance of a conviction is the sole means of individual advancement in the social hierarchy, and there is a compulsion to acknowledge this one faith, principles of genuine conviction are destroyed. Hypocrisy and cynicism rule the field and the longing for more credible theories grows.

Translated by V. Green

Notes

1. Leszek Kolakowski, *Der Mensch ohne Alternative* (Munich, 1960), pp. 8 ff.

2. *Op. cit.*, p. 9. Kolakowski says of the institutional Marxists: 'They have compromised the notion of Marxism, and identify it with their own way of thinking and with the activity of a bureaucratic authority', so that 'those who apply values in their work which Marx introduced into science are ashamed of the title "Marxist"' (pp. 13 ff).

3. From a private letter to the author.

4. J. G. Fichte, *Sämmtliche Werke*, 1845, vol. VI, pp. 365 ff.

Michael Traber

The African Church and African Socialism: The Tanzanian Model

THE significance of Tanzania lies in the fact that its government is making a specific effort to approach socio-political and economic problems with measures which should make it possible to effect a fundamental reorganization of Tanzanian society. Since the Church in Tanzania occupies a relatively strong position in the country, it seems meaningful to examine its relationship to contemporary politics, in which African socialism is the dominant factor. In this article I shall approach the problem as follows. Firstly, an outline of the basic ideas of Tanzanian socialism. I shall then discuss what is expected of the Church. A further point for consideration is the attitude of the Tanzanian hierarchy with specific reference to the Seminar Study Year organized in 1969 by the episcopal Conference. And finally I review the Tanzanian Church's approach to *ujamaa*.

THE BASIC IDEAS OF TANZANIAN SOCIALISM

In April 1962, i.e. five months after attaining independence, the Tanzanian head of state, Julius Nyerere, first declared his faith in African socialism. 'We in Africa need to be converted, as it were, to socialism. Socialism is as rooted in our past as democracy. The modern socialism which we represent is an extension and further development of our family system; society is to be seen as an extension of the family group.'[1] At that time President Nyerere did not have a definite socialist policy as such. However, he was already thinking in terms of a classless and therefore united society. For Nyerere even the one-party system in Tanzania is the manifestation in institutional form of a classless social structure.[2]

The key concept of Nyerere's socialism is the Swahili word *ujamaa*. Ujamaa is the principle governing the traditional African family, and signifies the family spirit or brotherliness. The tribes all lived according to this principle, though without expressing it in political terms. They lived together and worked together; this, for them, was the meaning of life. They shared the fruits of their combined efforts, the distribution following precise laws known and comprehended by all. Each member of the family should have enough to eat, simple but adequate clothing, and somewhere to sleep. Only when these basic needs of each individual had been fulfilled was it permissible to share out the surplus. The principle of *ujamaa* can be summarized in five points: (1) The equality of all; no one need exploit his neighbour, nor even wish to. (2) Mutual help; no one need starve if he is sick or if his supplies run out too soon after a bad harvest. (3) Community spirit; there is neither exploitation nor idleness in this society. Everyone contributes to the communal well-being according to his ability. (4) The obligation to work. Every healthy adult has the duty to work according to his strength and capilities. (5) Communal ownership of land. The land belongs to the community. Every member of the community has the right to the land, but no rights of ownership.

But Tanzanian socialism does not wish merely to return to the traditional forms of tribal society. Its aim is rather to apply the traditional values as a positive force in the new situation and to overcome inadequacies in the traditional system. This means, in effect, an extension of the idea of the family group to the nation as a whole, further still to the African continent, and finally to all mankind. Tanzanian socialism is attempting to apply modern technical and social achievements within the framework of traditional values in order to further socio-economic development.

Tanzanian socialism is not doctrinaire. Nevertheless, it has strongly moralistic overtones: 'If we claim that Marx and Lenin already had answers to all our questions, or rather, if we act as though Marx invented socialism, we are thereby disregarding the humane tradition of Africa and the universality of socialism.'[3] 'Socialism, like democracy, is not a system, but an attitude of mind. But this is not to say that social institutions and organisations are irrelevant. However, without the right attitude of mind institutions become alienated from their real purpose.'[4]

Nyerere explicitly *rejects* the *atheism* postulated by Marxist Communism. 'Socialism does not require its followers to become atheists. . . There is no conflict between socialism and Christianity, Islam or the other religions which acknowledge the equality of all men.'[5] For Nyerere the question of God is only relevant to socialism to the extent that it is one of the fundamental tasks of socialism to protect the dignity and esteem of the individual. In effect, this calls for a state which respects the religious convictions of *all* its citizens and is neither prejudiced for or against any specific religious group.

Finally, Tanzanian socialism should not be *repressive*. Democratic participation should be the determining force behind it. 'Socialist society cannot be created by force . . . The duty of the government and political leadership is not to compel the people, but to . . . sustain them.'[6]

NYERERE'S EXPECTATIONS OF THE CHURCH[7]

Nyerere, himself a Catholic, was continually astounded by the fact that the representatives of the Church were extremely reserved towards the policies of Tanzanian socialism, and apparently found difficulty in understanding his approach to various issues. Hence Nyerere felt the Church was adopting a negative attitude and was content to issue warnings against Communism. As a concrete example of this Nyerere cities the new Swahili edition of Pius XI's encyclical *Divini Redemptoris* (the 1937 encyclical against communism) published by the Tanzanian Episcopal Conference in 1970. Nyerere expects a less prejudiced attitude towards socialism and increased understanding for his policy of *ujamaa*. In his speech to the general Congress of the Maryknoll Sisters in New York on 16 October 1970, Nyerere exhorted Christians to adopt a more active rôle in the development of the Third World, and specifically in Tanzania. In Nyerere's view, the real problem of today's world is not poverty, but the division of mankind into poor and rich. The rich hold the lives of the poor in their power, and the rich nations determine the politics of less fortunate states. Nyerere therefore calls on the Church to 'acknowledge the necessity of a social revolution and to play a leading role in it'.[8] The Church must engage itself actively on the part of the poor. All too often the Church has identified itself with capitalism and feudalism. The Church today must 'acknowledge that the development of nations of necessity implies a rebellion.'[9] It should pull the poor out of their apathy and give them the help and encouragement they need, so that they no longer suffer injustice in silence. Above all, Nyerere expects the Church to 'challenge openly and emphatically all institutions and power groups which contribute to the continued existence of these physical and mental slums, regardless of the consequences for itself or its members'.[10]

For the Church's participation to be effective it is essential that it is prepared to collaborate with the people. Hence the Church should be poor like the poor, found co-operative villages, and collaborate with the state. In other words, it should be less concerned with running its own schools and hospitals and more concerned with participating in state institutions and with collaborating with its authorities. Nyerere calls to mind the revolutionary strength of the Christian faith. The Church should not be an 'element of constancy and permanence' but rather a 'source of innovation'.

ATTITUDES OF THE TANZANIAN HIERARCHY

The large religious communities are the only social groups in Tanzania apart from the one political party which carry any social and political weight. According to the census of 1967, of the 12.3 million inhabitants of Tanzania, 30.5% are Moslems and 30.6% Christians, of which about 1.2 million (10%) are Protestants and 2.5 million (20%) Catholics. The social position of the Church is further strengthened by its involvement in education and the health system.[11] Hence the question as to the attitude of the Christians towards socialism is not merely of pastoral and theological interest, but is also of significance in a wider political sense. Even before the days of independence, in their *Pastoral Letter for Christmas 1960,* the bishops made it emphatically clear that the Catholic Church was willing to play its part in building up the new Tanzania. They stressed the necessity for all groups to work loyally together. In its sphere of jurisdiction—the temporal, worldly—the state is autonomous. But even here it must fulfil the demands of the natural law, which includes the recognition of and support for religion. Although the Church is fundamentally of a religious, supernatural order, it nevertheless has its mission to fulfil within human society in this world. This consists above all in forming the consciences of its members who, being simultaneously citizens of a state, represent, so to speak, the extension of the Church's mission in the socio-political sphere.

In 1965 the Bishops' Conference of Tanzania published their *Rules of Conduct for those in the Service of the Church.* This document testifies to the efforts of Church leaders to establish a meaningful level of understanding with the authorities and party officials. Missionaries are called upon by the administrative council of the Episcopal Conference not to become involved in direct political activities, not to force western-style political opinions on the native population. They should, however, participate as far as possible in national development projects; but they should not launch any development project without first consulting with and obtaining the consent of the appropriate authority; but they should participate in any public meetings organized by either the party or the government. The administrative council also addresses a similar list of 'requests' to the representatives of the government, the party and the trade unions, with the intention of insuring that relations between these various bodies and the Church are based on mutual respect. One such request is that politicians should not expect or oblige the clergy to participate in national development projects or political meetings. Nor should the population be forced to act against their religious convictions.

In short, the Church's attitude towards the government is broadly speaking benevolent, but it sees no reason why the politics of the country should necessitate any profound reassessment of its own traditions and values.

In their pastoral letter of 1968, *The Church and Social Development in Tanzania,* the bishops took their first official stand on the Arusha declaration and to the socialist policies of the government. The Church's own contribution is only referred to indirectly here. This letter marked the centenary celebration of the Church's establishment in Tanzania and in it the bishops expressed their declared support for the 'spirit of brotherliness, of sharing, of service and hard work' as expounded in the Arusha declaration.[12] In particular they supported the participation of all in development work; the protection of the weak and handicapped, especially among the rural population; prophylactic measures against exploitation of any kind; development rooted in the people and their understanding of collaboration and solidarity; the aims of the policy of *ujamaa* according to which the principle of the family group will be applied to Tanzania as a whole, while at the same time respecting the individuality of the various different groups and tribes; and control of the most important means of production by the nation.

The dangers the bishops see in Tanzania's socialist policies are equally revealing. The following points are raised.

(1) The threat to the freedom of the individual through a too stringent control of the economy and other spheres of social life. (2) The threat to democracy through the concentration of too much power in the hands of one single group (the Unity Party (TANU). (3) The danger of the misuse of office by exploitation of the weakness, ignorance and fear of the ordinary people. (4) The danger to the dignity of womanhood by forcing the women to work so hard on the land that they have no time left for home and children, and by taking insufficient consideration of women's inherent qualities when assigning them to work on develop-

ment projects. (5) The danger of isolationism and disregard for the unity of mankind by interpreting the ideals of brotherliness and self-reliance in a nationalistic way.

In the pastoral letter of 1972, *Peace and Mutual Understanding,* the bishops concern themselves with several, in their view central, issues and critical aspects in the development of Tanzanian society. As they see it, what this society needs most is a deepening of mutual understanding. Faith in God can help not only the individual towards real progress; society, too, needs God, 'who is love'. For in a world without love men's lives are determined by mutual fear, self-seeking and violence. At the same time they call upon all Christians to participate intensively in developing the country, since the refusal of religious adherents to take part in this task is one of the reasons for the accusation that religion hinders progress. To prove that this reproach is without foundation the bishops then turn to the attitude of the Church and Christians towards development. Progress and the improvement of men's living conditions are a central issue in the Christian faith. Hence all Christians should participate with conviction in the planning and realization of development projects, and they should also collaborate with the government. Christians should give a living example of the power of true brotherly love. The teaching of the church stresses the dignity of labour, which it sees as the expression of man's responsibility for his life and health and of his participation in God's work of creation.

Another point raised in this letter concerns the rights of the individual and society respectively. On the one hand each individual is responsible towards society as a whole and should not limit himself to consideration merely of his own wellbeing. On the other hand, society, by means of its government and political leaders, has the responsibility to protect the freedom and dignity of the individual, to satisfy his justifiable expectations and needs, and in particular to respect his right to participate in open discussion and decision-making.

THE NATIONAL STUDY YEAR 1969: THE CHURCH IN TANZANIA TODAY

This 'Seminar Study Year' organized on behalf of the Episcopal Conference demonstrates the remarkable efforts being made by the church in Tanzania to reflect on its rôle in a rapidly changing country so that it can adapt itself to the new conditions. The National Seminar examined various different ways in which the central concept of Tanzanian socialism, *ujamaa,* could be seen in relation to the Church. They came to the conclusion that, given its mission, the Church should contribute to a deeper understanding of *ujamaa.* It could greatly increase the significance of the *ujamaa* outlook, in particulary by reflecting on her own early tradition. The spirit of selfless service and co-operation as well as its ideals of brotherly love and justice seem to indicate that the Church is well suited to be the conscience of a genuine *ujamaa* socialism. But first of all this ideal must manifest itself in the Church herself, in her teaching, in her services, and in the way Christians live together. It should be evident everywhere that the church exists for all men.

The Study Year wanted to obtain an official declaration of support for the *ujamaa* principles from the church leaders. But the suggestion of one subsidiary group went further still: they proposed that *ujamaa* should become the key concept of a total restructuring of the Tanzanian Church. "The church must rethink its structures in keeping with the historical and cultural conditions of its environment. The historical and cultural conditions of Tanzanian society are based on the idea of *ujamaa*.'[13] *Ujamaa* provides the church with an opportunity to realize its own ideal of human society, to bring its teaching closer to the people, so that men may experience it as a doctrine of liberation.

The general assembly of the National Study Year acknowledged the importance of *ujamaa* for a renewal of the Church in Tanzania appropriate to the given situation and time. But in view of the many unanswered questions and of the danger that the church might identify itself exclusively with one specific type of state or political ideology, the general assembly could not approve outright of the proposal of the *ujamaa* faction, and instead ordered a commission to be set up to study the matter. The National Seminar also raised the point that in the past the church leaders had shown too little interest in improving the standard of living of the rural population, and that insufficient emphasis had been laid on the Christian's duty to participate in public life and communal development. They therefore called on church leaders to show more concern for the community in general and in its development and to inform themselves about relevant government plans. Furthermore they demanded that the balance between expenditure on church buildings and on aid generally be re-examined and changed. And finally, they exhorted church leaders to participate personally if possible in development projects.

The National Seminar returned again and again to the theme of co-operation with other institutions and committees, and in particular, with the government. Through her readiness to co-operate the Church should prove once and for all that it really does serve all men; that it is not merely concerned with its own interests and those of its members; and that it does not use her assistance as a means to an end, i.e. to gain new converts. Basically, they demanded that the Church should give up the practice of setting up its own institutions in competition with those organized by the state, unless they fulfil some urgent need of the moment.

The Church should maintain its involvement in the *health sector*—in a subsidiary rôle—for as long as it is possible or necessary for it to do so. In the *education sector* stress is laid on the importance of good relations between the clergy and the teaching profession. The education act of December 1969 explicitly names religious education as one of the aims of education as a whole. As far as the *development sector* is concerned, the Church shows its willingness to co-operate chiefly by participating in state projects. The Church should only embark on its own schemes on the express wish of the authorities and on condition that these should be taken over by the local community as soon as possible. To date, the National Study Year has been the most important attempt of the Catholic Church in Tanzania to come to terms with changing conditions and political aims. The Study Year has instigated a process of reflection and radical re-evaluation of previously held attitudes.

THE TANZANIAN CHURCH'S ATTITUDE TO SOCIALISM

For a long time the Catholic Church in Tanzania, or at any rate a number of its leaders, equated the new socialist policies with the development of communism. Above all, their traditional understanding of socialism or communism as an atheistic, anti-religious ideology made it impossible for them to approve of Tanzanian socialism. The anti-religious statements of certain TANU politicians seemed to confirm this prejudice. However, lack of precise knowledge of *ujamaa* socialism and the resulting insecurity and discord among the bishops was probably a more decisive factor in creating their negative attitude. This would account for the astonishing fact that the Tanzanian Bishops' Conference of 1968 openly supported the aims of the Arusha declaration; that in 1970 they decided to publish a new Swahili edition of Pius XI encyclical against communism, and that in 1972, despite some reservations, they nevertheless called on the faithful to collaborate with the government.

In spite of previous indecision and scepticism, recent statements on the part of the Church seem to indicate a considerable degree of approval of the aims and basic concerns of *ujamaa* socialism. The Church has now come to the realization that *ujamaa* socialism fulfils many of its own precepts, such as concern for the individual and his freedom, the development of a fraternal society in which all men share equal esteem and equal rights. Similarly, the Church supports the socio-economic efforts being made to overcome poverty, disease and ignorance and is prepared to co-operate. It also welcomes the attempts being made to bring the benefits of development to all sectors of society, in particular to the rural population. The Church occupies an extremely privileged position with regard to this process. At present no other organization in Tanzania has at its disposal an equivalent body of trained men who are specialists in all the areas essential to the development of the country. The critical situation of Tanzanian socialism indicates that the *ujamaa* model is not threatened so much by socio-economic factors as by a negative attitude of mind. This is precisely where the Church can help. For its privileged position with regard to specialist knowledge combined with its basic mission and doctrines provide the Church with a unique opportunity for political involvement, which is 'not the only way but nevertheless an excellent way for Christians to live in active service of others'.[14] If this is to be achieved, the Church must identify herself, in the positive and not the exclusive sense, with *ujamaa* socialism. The Church cannot distance itself 'apolitically' from action without assuming a 'reactionary' or 'counterrevolutionary' function in Tanzanian socialism. The Church's support for the poor, the needy and the outlawed necessarily presupposes a political involvement. On one crucial point the Church will inevitably come into conflict with Tanzanian socialism, namely, on the question of the approval of violence as a means of liberation in southern Africa. This question is of immense significance in Tanzania's foreign policy, especially with regard to other African countries. To date, the question as to the legitimacy of violence has scarcely been mentioned in the Church's critical confrontation with *ujamaa* socialism. Although the Catholic Church is to a large extent in agreement with the basic concerns of *ujamaa* it remains politically reserved. Above all, it objects to the concentration of political power in the hands of one single party; to increasing state control over all spheres of public life; and to the restriction of the rights of the individual. It also has reservations towards a policy which in effect is reducing the principles of *ujamaa* to mere economic progress. And finally, the fear was expressed that the deliberate emphasis on national autonomy could lead to nationalism which would be in total contradiction to the ideal of universal unity and equality among men.

Nyerere's unremitting summons to participate in the socio-economic development of Tanzania seems to suggest that the Church is now playing the passive rather than the active role. She seems to lack initiative and solidarity. Nevertheless, one cannot overlook the fact that on the local level Christian communities are definitely providing the impulse necessary for a fundamental renewal of society. The *ujamaa* movement has shown the Church new possibilities of social reform to be effected at the deepest level of the social structure.

The fundamental importance of *ujamaa* socialism for the cultural, socio-economic and political development of Tanzania, and the Church's recognition of these concerns could lead to a renewal of the Church's own spiritual potential, structures and institutions. There are hopeful signs of the emergence of 'new ways of sharing in community'.[15] But the question still remains as to whether the efforts of the Tanzania Church within the context of *ujamaa* socialism are not doomed to failure unless action is taken on an international level, both in the ecclesiastical and political spheres.[16] In this respect the Tanzanian Church's support for *ujamaa* socialism must be seen as a problem of global dimensions. In any event, the Tanzanian Church has definitely begun the slow process of acknowledging *ujamaa* socialism as a concrete possibility for its missionary task in woking towards the universal shalom. It has taken up the offer Nyerere made when he said: 'I am giving the Christian churches a new chance to identify themselves with God's poor'.[17]

Translated by Sarah Twohig

Notes

1. A. H. Rweyemamu, 'Socialism in Operation' (Survey of Tanzania), *The Financial Times* (London) 9 December 1971.

2. Cf. A. H. Rweyemamu, *op. cit.*

3. J. K. Nyerere, *Freedom and Socialism* ('Introduction', p. 15).

4. *Ibid.* ('The Varied Paths to Socialism'), p. 309.

5. *Ibid.* ("Introduction").

6. *Ibid.* ("Socialism and Rural Development"), p. 356.

7. Cf. I. Peterhans, *Katholische Kirche und Sozialismus in Tanzania* (Freiburg i. Ue., 1974) (licentiate), pp. 44ff.

8. J. Nyerere, *The Speech to the Maryknoll Congress in New York on 16 October 1970*, Dar-es-Salaam, p. 18.

9. *Op. cit.,* p. 10.

10. *Op. cit.,* p. 14.

11. Cf. P. V. Dias, W. Küper and H. Weiland, *Die Entwicklungspolitische Bedeutung des christlichen allgemeinbildenden Schulwissens in Afrika,* 2 vols. (Freiburg, 1971).

12. Tanzania Episcopal Conference, *The Church and Developing Society of Tanzania: Message of the Bishops for the Centenary of the Church 1868–1968,* Ndanda, No. 4.

13. *Pastoral and Research Institute of Tanzania Bukumbi* (ed.). (1): cf. *idem, Seminar Study Year. The Church in Tanzania Today. Its tasks and Priorities:*

Summaries and Questions for Discussion, Mwanza, 1969;[1] (Findings of the SSY National Seminar (reproduced, Mann), 2.).

14. *Equality and Participation: Pope Paul VI's apostolic letter "Octogesima adveniens" to Cardinal Ray*, (Freiburg i. Ue., 1971), p. 60.

15. Cf. L. Gämperle in *Concilium* 9 (1973).

16. Cf. J. Amstutz, G. Collet and W. Zurfluh, *Kirche und Dritte Welt im Jahr 2000*, (Zurich, Einsiedeln, Cologne, 1974).

17. W. Bühlmann, 'Die Kirche als entwicklungsfördernder Faktor in Afrika', in: *Internationales Afrika Forum*. Ed. Europ. Institut für wirtschaftliche und soziale Fragen, Munich, 7 (1971), pp. 549–55, 554.

Nguyen Quoc-Hung

Church and Nation in Vietnam

RECENTLY, yet again, the Church in Vietnam has been the subject of a number of articles and commentaries, often mutually contradictory. Much depends on the extent of the involvement and sympathy of those who write to analyse that Church or to contribute to its formation. My own attitude is quite straightforward: I believe the Church will find its proper place in the new society of Vietnam and will be a valuable participant in it. To understand the hopefulness of the present situation it is important to take a thorough look at the past.

The Catholic Church was introduced into Vietnam along with gunpowder and spices, as a result of Alexander VI's bull, *Inter Caetera*, of 4 May 1493, empowering Portugal to conquer and evangelize the Lands of the East. The first missionaries, Dutch Jesuits, were received by the lords of Annam with a sympathy which varied according to the more or less regular arrival of ships bearing arms and ammunition. As the Portuguese Empire declined in the seventeenth century, the Society for Foreign Missions was established in Paris. Hoping for support from the Court at Versailles and from the East India Company, the new society replaced the Portuguese in 'undertaking the glorious design of converting the barbarians. Thus [the East India Company] wishes to sanctify its trade, enlarge the Church and enrich France' (Report of 14 March 1667 from Mgr Pallu, the first Bishop in Vietnam, whom the Company appointed its Recorder). In the eighteenth century, Vietnam was rent by internecine struggles between the Trinh and Nguyen dynasties; these were punctuated by popular uprisings led by a peasant from Tay Son, a certain Nguyen Hue. The Nguyen turned to the French, and allied themselves with the Bishop of Adran and Vicar Apostolic of the South, Mgr Pigneau de Béhaine, who negotiated for military help from France. The Court of Versailles was prevented from sending troops by political problems at home, so Mgr de Béhaine used the funds of the Paris Society for Foreign Missions, and called upon his friends to arm a fleet and enlist volunteers. Upon this, the Tay Son authorities became suspicious, and Christians—above all missionaries—were hunted down. Mgr Pellerin, Béhaine's successor, suggested to Napoleon III that he occupy Vietnam, assuring him that this step would have the support of the native Christians. On 31 August 1858 the French fleet bombarded Danang. Saigon fell on 18 February 1859. In 1867 the whole of Cochin-China became a French colony. Hanoi was taken in 1873. In 1883 Adminal Courtbet bombarded Hue, the capital. In 1884 all of Vietnam became a French possession.

Resistance was organized. Christians, looked on as allies of the invaders, were pursued and repressed. But French domination was reinforced, and with it the Vietnamese Church made rapid strides. In 1885 it numbered 600,000 believers: in 1945 there were 1,500,000. However it was not until 1933 that Rome appointed the first Vietnamese bishop; the second was in 1936 and the third in 1939. They were responsible for three rural dioceses, while fourteen others were entrusted to missionary bishops who represented 20% of the clergy. The colonial administration hastened to ask Paris to intervene to dissuade Rome from making these native appointments, since 'it will be hard for the Annamese bishop to stifle the impulsions of nationalism in his compatriots, when the development of ideas and affairs is doing so much to stimulate it' (Confidential report from the Governor General of Indo-China, 12 December 1934).

The resistance grew. On 2 September 1945, Ho Chi Minh declared the independence of Vietnam. On 23 September, Mgr Nguyen Ba Tong sent a message to Pope Pius XII, in the name of four bishops and a million and a half Vietnamese Catholics, begging for his blessing 'upon our independence, which Vietnam has just achieved, and will strive at all costs to maintain'. However, General Leclerc landed with his troops at Saigon, to 'win back the Empire'. On 4 November, the four Vietnamese bishops once again launched an appeal to Christians all over the world, to 'come to the aid of our beloved country, and spare us the horrors of war. Our country is now being invaded and is defending its independence, the cause of justice and of freedom'. None of the fourteen missionary bishops put his name to this appeal.

The French army was unable to make any progress: the enemy adopted guerrilla tactics which made them too elusive. So the 'anti-Communist crusade' began. De Lattre de Tassigny was encouraged by receiving the blessing of Pius XII in a Rescript from the Holy Office of 1 July 1949: 'I bless the French army that you command and represent, for it is defending Christian civilization in that part of the world'. Most of the Catholics joined the French to fight the Communists. The hierarchy of Vietnam, most of whose members were missionaries, sent out a joint Pastoral on 9 November 1951, forbidding Christians to collaborate with the Resistance. On 7 May 1954, the French army lost the battle of Dien Bien Phu and the Geneva Accords were signed, recognizing the independence, sovereignty and unity of Vietnam, which was to remain divided into two provisional zones in military terms until the general elections set for 1956. The Catholics in North Vietnam, urged on by their clergy, emigrated in vast numbers to the South—45% of the laity went, and 72% of the clergy.

The promised elections never took place, and Vietnam remained divided in two. French colonization came to an end, but the United States took over, putting in one compliant government after another, including two long dictatorships—one by the fervent Catholic Ngo Dinh Diem, and one by a convert Nguyen Van Thieu. The anti-Communist crusade gained ground. G.I.s—whom Cardinal Spellman christened 'soldiers of Christ'—occupied South Vietnam. And Vietnam became one vast field of experimentation, in which all the most sophisticated techniques were used to undermine society, materially and morally, from within. However the American venture also met with defeat: on 30 April 1975, all of South Vietnam was liberated, and Vietnam entered into a new phase of its history.

As the Church has grown in Vietnam, over almost five hundred years, there have been missionaries who have given their entire lives, willingly and devotedly, to serving the poor by bearing witness to the Christian Faith. However, certain features have not changed over that long period. First of all, the Christian Church was 'imported' into Vietnam in circumstances in which pastoral concern was closely identified with colonial conquest. This is not something peculiar to Vietnam: we find it frequently in the missionary history of other countries in Asia and Africa. However the Church in Vietnam has remained alien to the fortunes of the Vietnamese people. Furthermore, it has allied itself to the ruling power, both by totally rejecting the traditional values of the country, and by openly receiving privileges from the occupiers. Consequently it has passed on not the good news contained in the gospel message, but a totally different colonialist ideology arising out of a policy of expansion and invasion; and in the course of its development, it has created a new social class uprooted from its native soil, alienated from its own home and shaped by its opposition to the aspirations of the people as a whole. It is hardly surprising that the image of the Church came to be identified with that of the enemy to be repelled, especially since that enemy enforced with impunity a permanent oppression of injustice upon the country. It was in vain to preach love and human equality to those who had personal experience of such exploitation. The Church in Vietnam bears a heavy responsibility for its betrayal of Christ's message. For the Gospel is not neutral, and however minimally it is lived, it does not allow of deliberately siding with the oppressor. Christ came, incarnate in the human condition, to bring the light of love, justice and hope that the world's equivocation makes it all too easy to forget. The whole history of the Vietnamese people is a long story of liberation—the liberation of the weak from the yoke of the strong, of the poor from the yoke of the rich. But this is unhappily not the history of the Church in Vietnam, or at least not of the institutional Church. But that is a historical accident, rather than something inherent in the teaching of the Faith. And therefore Christians, when they saw things as they really were, and above all, when they were daily confronted with the realities of the situation, became aware where their duty lay.

It was this glaring contradiction that impelled some individuals among the people of God to re-read the history of their own Church, and be bold enough to call upon the Church to turn again to the gospel message. Mgr Nguyen Ba Tong and his three colleagues were outstanding—but theirs was not the only case. When resistance against the French first began, there were priests and laypeople who asked themselves the question—which is the side of the poor and the oppressed? They went so far as to join the maquis. At the point when Vietnam was being ravaged by bombs, and the hierarchical Church was turning a deaf ear to the appalling suffering of the people, a group of Christians in the South wrote an open letter to the Pope (12 August 1970) declaring that 'the major obstacle to peace in Vietnam is the Catholic Church' because 'the Church of Christ remains the one and only support of the present régime'. Other Christian groups were inspiring movements for peace, for combatting police repression, against corruption and against the collusion of the official Church with the aggressors. The hierarchy and the majority of the faithful had been silent for too long. There was silence where there should have been an outcry against injustice, and there were privileges gained by collaborating with the occupying power. The Church had been lulled to sleep by long years of anti-Communist propaganda and indoctrination. The occupiers used the mass media to forecast 'bloodbaths' following the arrivals of revolutionary troops, thus creating panic among the Catholic community; To such a point that Catholics forgot that those 'on the other side' were their own brothers and sons—not 'bloodthirsty devils, bent on exterminating all Christians'.

However, recalling what had happened in 1954, the Catholics did not seek exile. They stayed, despite all their doubts and apprehensions.

Mgr Nguyen Kim Dien in fact declared that his people stayed less from conviction than from a spirit of sacrifice, that they were prepared for martyrdom to 'carry on their pastoral work, if need be for imprisonment, for suffering or persecution'. And on 21 April 1975, Mgr Nguyen Van Binh, Archbishop of Saigon, published a statement to his flock, exhorting them to 'be ready—in the same spirit of resignation as Christ in the garden of Gethsemane—to drink the chalice sent by the Father . . . Christ gave his life for us, and we too must give our lives for our brothers'.

Yet Saigon fell—and there was no persecution, no martyrdom. The revolutionary government hastened to proclaim freedom of belief and a general amnesty. In the past the Vietnamese had been tolerant, and they endured patiently through the long struggle for national liberation. With the return of peace, enormous efforts had to be made to repair the colossal destruction left by the war, and to reconstruct a society in which all would be equally at home in a spirit of mutual help. There was simply no time to re-kindle hatred.

In this tremendous atmosphere of hard work and reconciliation among the people as a whole, Catholics at last awoke to the realization that they were also, and perhaps primarily, Vietnamese. The hierarchy were not slow to revise their attitude. Two weeks after his city was liberated, the Archbishop of Hue declared: 'There is nothing more important in this world than human life, and nothing is more important for a human being than freedom and independence. Independence is becoming a reality in the former capital, Hue. As for freedom, the FLN have solemnly guaranteed freedom to everyone, including freedom of religion for believers of all faiths'. The Archbishop of Saigon, too, spoke: 'Along with our fellow countrymen, we rejoice that there is peace, and we will take our part in the life of the community under the leadership of the provisional revolutionary government'. He was to spell out this change of policy more clearly in a pastoral letter of 2 September 1975: 'In society as we knew it before, money, unscrupulous greed, corruption and immorality were the idols worshipped by all. Now that society has been overthrown and those idols cast down; a new society is in the making. Our people are restoring human rights, they recognize the value and significance of work, so that we shall together create a just and fraternal society in which people can serve and assist one another, love one another like brothers, and live in unity and trust in the same household'. Once again the hierarchy of Vietnam evinced their supreme ability to adapt rapidly to all the changing circumstances of the world. They have kept intact their position of privilege in a socialist Vietnam, and most of the faithful have lined up obediently behind their pastors.

However, there is a minority of clergy and laity who had been working away for peace long before that, and are still committed without any great fanfare to the building up of the new society. It is upon these quiet workers for justice and the Gospel that hope for the future rests. They are people who do not turn the gospel message into something so spiritual that self-interest masquerades as unworldliness, but keep coming back to the Gospel as the light that illuminates their commitment of solidarity to the fortunes of mankind. The revolutionary authorities do not underestimate the positive contribution these Christians can make to national reconstruction. When he received the Catholic delegation led by Mgr Nguyen Van Binh in Hanoi on 20 September 1976, the Prime Minister, Pham Van Dong, assured the Archbishop of Saigon that he too read the Gospel regularly, and that he saw no contradiction between the teachings of Christ and the socialist line the country was pursuing—in other words caring for the poor and seeking the happiness of all. And he added: 'If you read the Gospel, you must read it as it really is, not selectively'.

The clergy were invited to share in the activities of national life. Three priests—the Rev Vo Thanh Trinh, Chan Tin, and Ho Hue Ba—took part in the conference for the Reunification of Vietnam held in Ho Chi Minh City from 12 to 25 November 1975. Some priests also offered themselves for election to the People's Assembly, among them the Rev Chan Tin, editor of the Catholic review *Dung Day* (the first unofficial journal given a licence to publish) and the Rev Nguyen Cong Minh, editor of the Catholic weekly *Cong Giao va Dan Toc* (which was the second).

There have been other instances of the same kind. In the present situation, Catholics should have no special problem in becoming integrated into national life. They are subject to the same discomforts as all the rest of the Vietnamese people in this period of socialist construction, social reorganization and economic recovery. For the independence that has been won back in years of fighting is still fragile. The effects of the moral disintegration brought about by the war are still with us, and our former aggressors never miss an opportunity to cause trouble and threaten that independence. Nor is the Christian community exempt from this temptation. The incident of the parish of Vinh Son, where the priests organized 'popular forces for the reconquest of our country' in opposition to the régime was a typical hangover from the Church's long anti-Communist past.

Such, in brief, is the picture of the Catholic Church at this juncture in Vietnamese society. It is apparently very far from being a persecuted Church. But of course the question is not whether or not Vietnamese Catholics have freedom of religion: the real question is still whether

Catholics are capable of total fidelity to the commands of the Gospel, capable, that is, of living the good news authentically in their own lives among their fellows, and working effectively with them to rebuild a juster society; capable, in short, of being true disciples of Christ and true citizens of Vietnam.

The situation of the Catholic community in Vietnam can be looked at from various points of view, but this twofold demand means that one cannot have a proper understanding of it without actually being involved in its life, experiencing both the difficulties and the advantages. Vietnamese Catholics are at long last following the recommendations of Vatican II. Conceptualizing theology—even the theology of liberation—has never been their strong point. They are fully occupied in living a very difficult life. By practising their faith, they may one day succeed in being liberated from a particular theology. That is one way of doing things.

Translated by Rosemary Middleton

Fernando Castillo

Christians for Socialism in Chile

THIS article does not claim to reconstruct the history of the Christians for Socialism (CFS) in Chile,[1] which would involve analyzing the period of Popular Unity, but only to draw attention to some aspects and questions arising from this experience.

CHRISTIANS WHO OPT FOR SOCIALISM

The CFS movement started in Chile at the beginning of the period of the government of Popular Unity. In April 1971 a group of eighty priests from working class areas held a meeting, which produced a resolution expressing their commitment to the development of Socialism as it was then taking place in Chile. This unleashed an intense polemic discussion in the Chilean Church. The explicit choice of socialism by a group of priests meant a decisive step in breaking a whole network of socio-political positions which placed Christianity in natural opposition to socialism and set the Church in an alliance of complicity with the dominant classes.

This choice was not one separate act born of a particular juncture in the history of Chile: on the contrary it expressed—in a more overtly political manner—a basic choice which had been growing in the Latin American Church through various groups (generally of priests) and through the silent mass of Christians who were gradually taking up a more radical political commitment to the liberation of the working classes. In the year following its initiation, CFS organized the 'first Latin American meeting of the CFS' (April 1972) inviting participation by similar groups from other countries. The organization of the meeting presupposed a common experience throughout the whole continent.[2]

This was the basic reason for its deep repercussions; it was a moment of reflection on a practice that had already become a reality and was looking for ways in which to express itself. It is essential to understand this continental dimension in order to realize the strength of the Chilean movement and its conviction of belonging to the wider history of liberation of the Latin American peoples. Also the choice made by CFS in Chile is the result of a long process of maturation closely related to the political and social development of the country. During the sixties the dependent capitalist system clearly showed its own limits; for large sections of the population socialism appeared the only way out of the situation of underdevelopment and dependence. In this general framework the experience of the Democratic-Christian government in Chile (1964–70) played a decisive part in radicalizing Christian sections of the community. In a retrospective analysis CFS characterized this experience as 'Christian Reformism'—apparently a halfway house between capitalism and Socialism but in fact allied to the conservative forces in the country.[3] The failure and contradictions of Christian Reformism led them to seek other political courses to realize their commitment to the liberation of the working classes. It became more and more common for Christians to belong to socialist organizations.

The choice made by CFS was its particular way of choosing the side of the poor and the oppressed. The declaration of 'the eighty' stated: 'the basic reason for this commitment is faith in Jesus Christ, deepened, renewed and embodied in our historical circumstances. Being Christian is being one with the others, being one with the others in this moment in Chile means taking part in the historical course traced by its people'. Christians who take this radical approach understand that solidarity with the poor has to mean taking the political consequences. Political praxis shows in this way that 'the poor' are not an anomalous phenomenon but that the essence of capitalist society consists in there being 'poor' and those who oppress them. The poor become not individuals but social classes exploited by others and the relationship between rich and poor is one of domination, with the oppressed struggling to liberate themselves. What emerges is that the oppressed are involved in a structural conflict with the dominant classes—one that cannot be resolved through verbal conciliation—and that 'the Christian' is not excused from this conflict. Experience of conflict at this level is decisive for Christians: they come to realize that taking the side of the poor is taking the side of one class and participating in its struggle. The choice made by Christians—particularly by priests—originally took the form of material solidarity: sharing poverty in conditions of life, manual labour etc., but this experience of turning toward the world of the poor demanded a practical radicalization: sharing too in their struggles and hopes, taking part in their organizations and taking on their class interests and their political project of liberation. But CFS in Chile went further than this in insisting that its actions were autonomous: that is they did not necessarily stem from Christian principles and did not purport to lead to a 'Christian socialism'—which would be a project of their own—but to be incorporated in the socialist movement as the one and only project of the workers. In the discussion aroused by CFS the question of what model of socialism they were choosing was often asked.[4] This question, however, sometimes implies a misreading of the historico-particular nature of their choice. Socialism is basically a struggle to overcome capitalism and it takes on its particular form in the specific struggles of different peoples against capitalism. One does not choose a pre-established model antedating praxis, nor is it legitimate to try to impose schematic forms on the construction of socialism in this way, nor to claim that Christians should have to set conditions for their commitment to the socialist movement.

So CFS on the one hand underlined the autonomy of its praxis, which followed its proper political rationale; on the other, it underlined the relationship between its praxis and faith. Faith and evangelical commitment to the oppressed took a concrete form in its choice of socialism. If one sets aside the tendency to use faith as a legitimization of political praxis (which would be to deny the latter its autonomy) and the tendency to see faith as a simple motivation behind praxis (which would be the internal relationship of both), this double emphasis basically means posing the question of a new relationship between reason and faith on the level of praxis: as practical political reason and as a faith that is praxis. Criticism of a particular rationality—the one ruling in capitalist society—leads one to seek a new practical rationality. In this way too, understanding the faith in the field of praxis leads one to criticize forms of religious experience that deny the practical commitment to liberation.

THE IDEOLOGICAL STRUGGLE

The praxis of CFS was situated basically on the level of ideological struggle. This did not mean standing apart from the political field but rather the contrary. One should not have a partial idea of ideological struggle: in one way or another the whole complexity of the class struggle goes through an ideological struggle. This was particularly important in Chile due to the characteristics of Chilean life. The forces of Popular Unity had managed to become the government but not to hold sufficient power in the State to realize and consolidate a transformation of the structures of the country in a socialist direction;

Chilean life still continued with its juridico-political institutionalization and a broad framework of ideological pluralism. This meant that an ideological consensus was necessary to create a new set of institutions. The opposition used these same features to play a double game: relying on the institutions and ideological freedom while preparing a blow that would suppress them. In this context Christianity and the Church were elements that the bourgeoisie could try to mobilize against socialism; in another historical context they would have managed to do it. The obvious position of the Christian seemed to be, sooner or later, one of opposition to socialism. The dominant classes would undoubtedly try to bring about a confrontation. It was here that CFS played an extremely important role. Its only public existence—as an organization of Christians who committed themselves unambiguously to the particular form of socialism operating in Chile—was a pointer to the fact that the monopolization of Christianity by the dominant classes was about to be broken, as was its intention to use Christianity against the socialist revolution. The ruling classes could work on an ideological base which they themselves had worked out and imposed on the consciousness of the people, which made it a relatively simple matter to mobilize Christianity in a reactionary direction; socialism could be made out to be the associate of violence and hatred, over-riding basic human and Christian values, upsetting the established order, bringing atheism and religious persecution. So CFS through its actions had to work for a transformation of this ideological substratum. The ideological struggle had to go much deeper than merely making an 'act of presence' in the socialist revolution and bearing public witness to their commitment to it; it had to be an on-going activity designed to create a new consciousness among Christians and to overthrow the ideological barriers to their participation in the process of liberation, barriers which had been erected by the oppressors in the name of Christianity.

The ideological struggle in this sense was not designed to impose new forms of religious consciousness on the people but to act as a trigger for the people to articulate and discover their own Christianity as a dimension of the consciousness of liberation that it was gradually acquiring. The magnitude and importance of the ideological struggle was more and more clearly seen in CFS. The assumption of such tasks meant inevitably that they had to organize themselves and assure themselves channels of communication. This requirement led to the group of eighty forming the 'CFS Secretariat' and later to setting up the structure of a movement.

However, on the level of the ideological struggle there was a certain amount of opposition between immediate tasks imposed by the urgency of the various political events that were taking place in Chile and longer term objectives such as the formulation of a set of Christian symbols firmly linked to the practice of liberation. The short-term tasks meant the movement had to publicize its Christian commitment continually and to insist at the same time on its compatibility with Christianity, while not allowing it to question deeply the ideologized forms of Christianity. The immediate task meant exalting the role of public declarations and of the directing committee, while the task of arousing a new Christian consciousness required a long, slow process at a more basic level. Faced with this alternative, CFS in Chile—in the same way as many other organizations which have been forced by the speed of events—gave greater emphasis to fulfilling its immediate tasks.

CFS AND THE AUTHORITY OF THE CHURCH

CFS never cast doubt on the fact that it belonged to the Church, although it never considered itself a 'church movement'; it never called the necessarily institutional nature of the Church into question, although it never sought to define its own place within that institution. Its relationship with the institutional Church was dialectical and one of conflict: dialectical because it declared its identity with the Church while necessarily distancing itself from the Church and contradicting some of its edicts, which in itself brought it into conflict with authority. A central point in this conflict was its particular conception of the political nature of the Church. CFS was born as a group of priests and—although many lay people later became part of it—it kept this characteristic, at least to a certain extent. This characteristic was in fact determined by the role culturally assigned to the priest in Chile and in Latin America in general; a group of lay people would never have managed to get themselves recognized publicly as 'Christians' for socialism. Given this fact, the hierarchy objected and continued to object that CFS unjustifiably involved the Church in politics, thereby endangering Christian unity. This argument of course supposed the a-political nature of the Church and of Christianity, which was something that CFS could not accept; for them the Church had possessed and still possessed political power, de facto; the problem was not whether the Chruch should involve itself in politics but in what direction it was going to use the political influence it in fact had: either for or against the popular movement. Without trying to reconstruct the discussion now one must recognize that the problem of the political nature of the institutional Church takes on a new dimension in relation to socialism; 'political' is no longer defined exclusively in terms of 'power' but in relationship to the problem of the transformation of society. Emphasizing the political nature of the Church was no longer necessarily defining it as a 'power' centre but stressing its participation—positive or negative—in the process of building socialism as a particular process of liberation in Chile. This political nature would then imply even the loss of 'power' by the Church.

The conflict with the hierarchy, however, gave rise to some tendencies within CFS to accentuate its conflict with the Church. This brought with it a danger of confusing the real enemy and losing sight of the real goals of the movement; the danger of making an almost mechanical transference of the class struggle to the inner life of the Church. This led to a tendency to overlook the fact that the difference between classes did not coincide with the authority structure of the Church and that there was also a struggle within the hierarchy between those who wished to see the Church in the forefront of opposition to the government and those who took a positive view of the road to socialism or at least of some aspects of it. The conflict tended to become gradually more acute; there were moments of tension during the organizing of the Latin American meeting, although the official position of the hierarchy was to recognize the right of Christians to meet freely in order to think. Finally, on 13 September 1973—two days after the coup—when not only CFS but all the forces of the Left were scattered, the Bishops approved a document clearly reprimanding CFS, forcing the group to choose between its political activity and belonging to the Church.

AFTER THE MILITARY COUP

The brutal nature of the military coup in Chile is well-known. In the months that followed it, CFS—now operating clandestinely—decided to dissolve itself as a movement. The new conditions of dictatorship and extreme repression of the people—and very soon general scarcity and hunger—imposed new tasks and forced it to seek new ways of showing its solidarity with the people. Many members of CFS had to flee from Chile and their experience has contributed to the formation or support of groups of Christians for socialism in other countries. Others who stayed in Chile joined church organizations and structures through which solidarity could be practised in a more effective and broader way and a ray of hope in the consciousness of the people maintained. The political conditions in Chile put off the problem of socialism as a direct objective and set other tasks and priorities: defence of human rights and organization of at least minimal help to the oppressed. These conditions mean that solidarity is no longer sharing merely the hopes of the people but also their history of suffering and their present downcast state. Through this Christians are constructing a common history with the people. But the new political situation in Chile does not mean the end of socialist aims; on the contrary, it shows the viability of socialism as the only way of liberation from the extreme oppression at present in force. Because of this, CFS is still a viable movement and remains an open problem for the Church in Chile.

Translated by Paul Burns

Notes

1. For a history of CFS in Chile, see P. Richard, *Cristianos por el Socialismo: Historia y documentación* (Salamanca, 1976).

2. *Primer Documento de Trabajo*, conference document produced by CFS after the first Latin-American meeting. Text of the international edition (Santiago, 1972), pp. 14–27.

3. See 'Informe de delegación de Chile al Primer Encuentro Latinoamericano de CpS', in *op. cit.*, pp. 89–92.

4. See particularly, Chilean Bishops, *Evangelio, política y socialismos: Documento de trabajo* (Santiago, 1971). CFS replied with another document, entitled 'Reflections on the working document', published in *Cuadernos de la Fundación Manuel Larraín Talca* (1971).

Ivo Lesbaupin

The Latin American Bishops and Socialism

INTRODUCTION

OVER the last two decades the attitude of the Latin American bishops has been characterized by a progressive taking stock of the misfortunes of the Latin American people, of the situation that has been called a situation of injustice and one which demands urgent transformation. In the sixties the appeal to development predominated, with a request for basic and deep reform. Gradually, however, they came to realize that the situation was one of external and internal dependence, which did not leave room for development and which therefore required a process of liberation.

The evolution of the bishops' thought can be seen to have taken place through successive stages. It began with a realization of the increasing poverty of the masses, of glaring social inequalities and of injustices. This realization made them insist on the need for ever more radical change. In the beginning there was no very clear appreciation of the causes of the situation. They spoke of the 'abuses' of capitalism, of some faults of the economic system which had to be corrected, of the necessary social role of private property. But the continuation and even aggravation of the exploitation of the people led them to a deeper inquiry into the causes. This led to a realization that it is capitalism itself, the very socio-economico-politico-cultural system in which we are living, that is the main cause of existing poverty and injustice. Private ownership of the means of production is the determining factor in the expropriation of the Latin American people. What is needed therefore is a new world, a new society, one that breaks with the structures of the present system and makes it possible for men to live and enjoy the benefits of their work, for brotherhood to reign between them. The next stage then was to adopt the language of socialization and to come to appreciate the values existing in socialism. From this point on there was a clear affirmation that the only way out is that of socialism: only social ownership of the means of production will lead to an effective change in society and create conditions necessary for the liberation of the Latin American people. Let us go on then to examine the course of this evolution through the texts.

THE SITUATION OF INJUSTICE IN LATIN AMERICA

'There have been many studies made on the situation of the Latin American countries. All of them describe the poverty which marginalizes huge groups of human beings. This poverty as a collective fact is an injustice that cries out to the heavens'.[1] So begins the first document of the Second General Conference of the Latin American Episcopate held in Medellín in 1968. 'Latin America is in many parts in a situation of injustice that can be called *institutionalized violence*', since through faults in the industrial and agricultural structure, in national and international economies, in cultural and political life, 'whole populations deprived of the necessities of life live in a dependence that robs them of all initiative and responsibility and also of all possibility of cultural development and access to a social and political career, which is a violation of basic human rights'.[2] Since Medellín in particular, every document issued by the Latin American bishops makes reference to, analyzes and denounces the injustices practiced against the people: imperialism, neo-colonialism, structural marginalization of the great population masses, the multi-national corporations, an elitist structure based on the exploitation of the majority, etc.[3]

One can see that the bishops are gradually moving from an appreciation of the injustices to a quest for their causes. There is hardly any talk of hunger, infant mortality etc., but of injustice, of the 'situation of sin', which implies human causality: there are people who are interested in the maintenance of this situation, there are economic, social and political structures that generate this situation. These structures need to be analyzed.

The way to find the causes starts with a critique of capitalism. In the beginning the causes are attributed to faults in capitalism, to 'abuses' of the system; the capitalist system can still be good once its faults are corrected: 'without doubt not everything is evil in liberalism or in capitalism. Let us remember therefore the criticisms that the Church has made of the abuses deriving from both doctrines for more than a century'.[4] In another document it is affirmed that, 'the Church recognizes "surplus" or "profit" as fully legitimate short-term aims of economic activity, but profit cannot be the only motive for economic growth nor the final criterion of the social utility of an enterprise'.[5] In order to put right the innumerable problems seen in the system, a whole series of reforms in the field is suggested, affecting the structure of companies and law, without particularly looking for a change of system.

Private property is seen as one of the basic causes of the injustices. The bishops in the first documents after Medellín have not reached the stage of proposing its abolition, but call attention to its correct understanding: 'By its faith in private property the Church believes that this has to be admitted not only in theory but also in practice and therefore it defends the need for seeking every possible way of extending private property to all social classes. However, ownership of the means of production and the goods of the earth, however much this is defended under an apparent juridical legality, could be a real assault on the right of property if it means that large sectors of the population are deprived of the exercise of their natural right to possess what is necessary for themselves and for their families. This is the source of the Church's teaching on the social function of private property. The earth and its goods were created by God above all for all men'.[6]

THE CAPITALIST SYSTEM—THE CAUSE OF INJUSTICES

The search for the causes of oppression and exploitation does not end there. There is a gradual realization growing steadily clearer that abuses and faults are not accidents of capitalism capable of being corrected: they are the natural fruits of its very essence—'this situation, of poverty more marked in the North East, far from being the inevitable effect of nature's insufficiency, is above all the result of a process determined by the will of men who are committed to international capitalism'.[7] Our situation of poverty and under-development, of hunger and the exploitation of the people is a 'sub-product of capitalist development in Western society'.[8]

'The socio-economic system and the political and cultural situation of our people is a challenge to our Christian conscience. Malnutrition, infant mortality, prostitution, illiteracy, unemployment, cultural and political discrimination, exploitation and the growing inequality between rich and poor, together with numerous other consequences, are the characteristics that make the situation in our country one of institutionalized violence. The rich become richer and the poor become steadily poorer through the enslaving process of economic concentration inherent in the system. Furthermore, the need for repression in order to guarantee the functioning and security of the capitalist system becomes steadily more imperious and more inexorable in its hold on the institutions that make up the legislature, in the de-politicization of rural and urban syndicates, in the persecution of student leaders, and finally in the censorship system; through the means taken to persecute workers, peasants and intellectuals, through the penalties inflicted on priests and militants of the Christian Churches, all this allied to all sorts of imprisonment, torture, mutilation and even assassination . . . the injustice generated by this situation is based on the capitalist ownership of the means of production, which inevitably gives rise to a class society marked by discrimination and injustice'.[9]

Therefore there is an urgent need 'to change the intrinsically human structure of this system', which considers profit as the essential motor of economic progress, competition as the supreme economic law and private ownership of the means of production as an absolute right. It is not enough to say that this scenario, which corresponds to the era of liberal capitalism, does not exist any longer. Whatever the new name or the new clothes it may adopt, the scenario is still real and it is of the very essence of capitalism that it should remain so.[10]

Injustices are no longer presented as mere facts or natural calamities; the root cause of the evil is found in private ownership of the means of production. The time for talking of the social function of this ownership is past; what is needed now is its abolition: 'we have to overcome capitalism, this is the greater evil, the accumulation of sin, the withered root, the tree that produces the fruits that we know: poverty, hunger, destitution, death for the great majority. This is why private ownership of the means of production (of factories, of the land, of business, of the banks, of sources of credit) has to be abolished'.[11] 'Private property?', asks Dom Helder Camara: 'who cannot see that Christians in this respect have abandoned the Fathers of the Church and found a divine right to private property when what is of divine right is that property should be extended to all and not constitute odious and oppressive monopolies?'[12]

THE NEED FOR RADICAL CHANGE: LIBERATION

We therefore need to set out for a new world. We live in an age, 'full of desire for total emancipation, for liberation from every servitude, for personal maturity and collective integration. In this we see the forewarnings of the painful birth of a new civilization . . . We cannot fail to see vestiges of the image of God in man appearing with a potent dynamism in this increasingly tenacious and urgent will for transformation'.[13] The situation of the people requires: 'global, audacious, urgent and deeply renewing transformations'.[14] If earlier documents had called for partial and sectoral reforms they now require structural change, global transformation, true revolutions: 'as long as everyone insists on acting for himself our task is to witness that this society is in need of a revolution: a revolution in truth and in justice, a revolution in charity'.[15]

It is not possible to achieve this new world simply through a process of development within the structures of capitalism, since this would be development of underdevelopment. What is needed is a break—a liberation. This is what the Peruvian bishops say on the subject: 'to build a just society in Latin Amercia and in Peru requires liberation from the present situation of dependence, oppression and exploitation, in which the great majority of our people live. Liberation will mean on the one hand a break with all that keeps man unable to realize himself as man on a personal and community level; and on the other hand, the building of a new, more human and more brotherly society . . . the relationship between eschatology and politics arises from the effort to form a historical project which will be liberating; that is, which will strive for the advent of a society based on justice, fraternity and solidarity, and of a truly new man'.[16]

The people must be the principal agents of this liberation and of this building of a new society: 'let all Peruvians be authors and architects of their destiny. Our liberation requires an order in which men will no longer be objects but agents of their own history'.[17] 'The people must have real and direct participation'.[18] 'We are convinced that this new world will be built above all through the work of those who today are despised, through the work of our people'.[19] This is one of the most significant evolutions in the thought of the Latin American bishops. For a long time all hope of change had been based on the business owners, the rich classes and the centres of power, but now the bishops no longer call on the dominators, but on the people themselves, considering them as protagonists of their liberation: 'in the first place the poorest peoples and the poorest among the people have the task of bringing about their own advancement'.[20] Social change is not merely a revolution made for the people but the people themselves—and particularly the exploited and unjustly marginalized peasant and urban proletarian sectors—are those who have to be agents of their own liberation. This participation requires the oppressed to realize the situation of injustice.[21] The Church will take steps to bring this about.[22]

We need to build a different world. What will this world be like? 'We want to see a world in which the fruits of work will belong to all. We want to see a world in which people will work, not in order to get rich, but in order that all should possess the necessities of life: enough to eat for their health, a house, education, clothes, shoes, water and light. We want to see a world in which money is placed at the service of men and not men at the service of money. We want to see a world in which all will be able to work for all, not a divided world in which everyone works only for himself. Therefore, we want to see a world in which there will be only one people with no division between rich and poor. We want to see a world in which everyone will do all he can for the common good'.[23]

VISIONS OF A NEW SOCIETY: SOCIALISM

The dramatic denunciation of injustices, the criticisms of capitalism, the denunciation of private property and the perception of the need for overall and urgent structural reforms led inevitably to the need to choose a new system. This system emerged as socialism.

The choice was neither immediate nor unanimous. At first socialization was seen as being the way: 'socialization understood as socio-cultural process of personalization and growing solidarity leads us to think that all sectors of society—in the case in question principally the socio-economic sector—should overcome their antagonisms through justice and brotherhood and so become agents of national and continental development'.[24] The term 'socialism', however, was already beginning to appear: 'this is why so many Christians today recognize a number of the aspirations they encourage in themselves in the name of faith in socialist currents of thought'.[25] This does not mean accepting any type of socialism: 'there are in fact many types of socialisms'; among these there are some that are compatible with the Christian Spirit, that is in which the State does not become an uncontrollable, dictatorial power.[26] Some documents show serious reservations about socialism but recognize that in some of its forms it possesses acceptable values that are compatible with faith.[27] The greatest reservations in these documents are with regard to Marxist socialism. They hold that Marxism is basically atheistic and that this form of socialism is anti-religious, while at the same time it allows an all-powerful State to oppress individuals. Despite this, they recognize that at the origins of socialism is, 'an aspiration to justice, a desire to improve the condition of the poor, a will to control the power of money and a desire for equality', which are Christian values to be found in the Bible and in the Gospels, which are our own values, which cannot be denied merely because others take them as theirs.[28] We should not lose sight of the fact that whenever a document criticizes Marxism, it also criticizes capitalism and in particular the use of anti-communism as a means of maintaining 'structures that are institutionalized and secular violence, since they rest on the privileges of the few maintained by the poverty of millions'.[29] Another aspect that causes a certain amount of reservation in some documents is the possibly violent character of the changes needed: 'no one should be surprised if we strongly re-affirm our faith in the fruitfulness of peace. This is our Christian ideal; violence is neither Christian nor evangelical'.[30] At the same time there is a realization that it was not the violence of the oppressed that came first: 'it should not then surprise us that in Latin America there is a growing temptation to violence (against institutionalized violence). We must not abuse the patience of a people that has for so many years borne a condition that anyone with a greater appreciation of human rights would find difficult to accept'.[31] Violent reaction is the result of a situation of domination and dependence in which the oppressed peoples live and in which they will continue to live if the necessary changes are not brought about.[32]

Despite such reservations, other documents are coming all the time closer to socialism: 'the word "socialism" sounded terribly wrong to us formerly, today there is a change of tone and we speak of the process of socialization. The French bishops have recently published a letter in which they state that socialism, providing that it respects personal rights, is in many ways more in conformity with and closer to the Gospel than capitalism, which is based on personal self-interest'.[33] 'I consider that a socialist system is closer to Christian principles of true brotherhood, justice and peace . . . whatever form of socialism we adopt, one or another has to be the line for Latin America to follow. For my own part I believe it should be a democratic socialism'.[34] The bishops of the Third World have said: 'the Church can only rejoice at the appearance of a social system closer to the morality of the prophets and the Gospel. Christians have a duty to show that true socialism is Christianity lived fully in a true sharing of goods and in basic equality. Far from rejecting it, we should welcome it with joy as a form of social life better adapted to our time and more consonant with the spirit of the Gospel'.[35] The episcopal documents show an increasing insistence on the need to base action on a scientific analysis of reality.[36] This scientific understanding of the situation leads them to see that there is no other way out: 'for our under-developed world there is no way out except that of socialism understood as social ownership of the means of production'. Socialism is liberation from imperialism, from colonialism in all its forms—cultural, economic and political; it is a radical change of structures.[37]

The suggestion of socialism is a direct result of the criticism of capitalism: 'there follows the need to replace private ownership of the means of production and to promote social ownership which is a more effective response to the meaning of human work and the common destiny of goods'.[38] The Church should commit itself to support and contribute to 'achievement of our own way to a socialist society'.[39] The task is not seen as one of, 'building a Christian socialism, since this would be to absolutize socialism and relativize Christianity, just as in the past we absolutized western society or democracy or humanism or religion itself by calling them Christian, and thereby relativized and diminished Christianity, the vital presence of God in history'.[40]

If the basis of capitalism is private ownership of the means of production, then a new society can only be based on social ownership of the means of production, which is the basis of socialism: 'the dominated class has no other way in which to free itself except through the long and difficult course it has undertaken in favour of the social ownership of the means of production. This is the main basis of the gigantic historical project for the overall transformation of present-day society towards a new society in which it will be possible to create objective conditions where the oppressed can recover their stolen humanity, throw the rags of their suffering on the ground, overcome class antagonisms and finally win their freedom. The Gospel calls all Christians and all men of goodwill to an engagement in its prophetic current. Christian hope, which shows the way to a new humanity reconciled to itself and at peace with the universe, does not allow us to remain inert, passively waiting for the time when all things will be restored, 'the final liberation from captivity to participate in the glorious freedom of the Children of God', but requires our wakeful and alert presence, capable of putting the promise of the ressurrection to work in history, of identifying the first signs of the new humanity of the future'.[41]

CONCLUSION

The choice of socialism as seen in the episcopal documents is the result of long years of living with poverty, with the exploitation of the people and constant frustration of popular aspirations. It became clearer when analysis showed capitalism to be at the root of the oppression of the poor. There was then a rapid passage from seeing private ownership of the means of production as the basis of the existing evil to the need to move towards social ownership of these means. Socialism showed itself as the possibility of building a more human, more just and more fraternal society.

This choice is shared by many bishops and several groups of bishops. The Latin American episcopate taken as a whole is less precise. It denounces existing injustices as the effects of capitalism, it perceives some of their causes and criticizes many aspects of capitalism, it feels the need for deep changes, it proposes a more just society in which the existing evils will be overcome, but it does not know precisely what type of society this should be, and often prefers to accuse both capitalism and socialism, opting for a third way which would seem to contain elements of both systems. Those bishops who have already opted for socialism criticize this position as being in practice another way of maintaining the status quo: without striking at the basis of the old society no change will succeed in replacing the existence of exploiters and exploited.[42] They believe that change will in any case come of its own accord: 'without denying that restrictions can achieve their objective for the time being, it is nevertheless impossible for the dynamic social advance to be contained since this is sweeping across the world and sooner or later will sweep away any unstable situation with it'.[43]

Translated by Paul Burns

Notes

1. 'The Church in the Present Transformation of Latin America in the light of the Council'; references are to the Portuguese version published by Vozes (Petropolis, 1969)—referred to as *Medellín, Justice,* 1, p. 41.

2. *Medellín, Peace,* 16, p. 55.

3. Communiqué drafted by the Representative Commission of the National Conference of Brazilian Bishops (CNBB), sent to the 1971 Synod, published in SEDOC *(Servico de Documantacão)* n. 41 (1971), p. 403. Other resolutions of National Conferences also published in SEDOC, various nos., 1968–71. Cf. also *Medellín, Justice* 1,2.3.16; *Peace*, 15, 16, pp. 41, 42, 47 and 55.

4. Chilean Bishops, 'Evangelio y paz', in SEDOC 90 (1976), p. 982.

5. Pastoral letter of the Mexican bishops, in *ibid*, p. 875. For the partial failures of capitalism, cf. also *Medellín, Justice*, 2, 10, pp. 41–5; 'Evangelio y paz', *loc. cit.*, pp. 977–82; Chilean bishops, 'Fe cristiana y actuación política', in SEDOC 74 (1974), p. 283; 'Evangelio, política y socialismo', *ibid*. pp. 1451–66; 'La iglesia en Bolivia', *ibid.*, p. 1388; pastoral letter of the Mexican bishops, *ibid.*, pp. 867–81.

6. Documents and 'declarations' by various national hierarchies published in SEDOC: bishops of Honduras in n. 33; of Colombia in n. 39; of the bishops of the West-Centre of Brazil in n. 69; of Honduras in n. 56; of Argentina in n. 57; D. Pedro Casaldaliga, bishop of S. Félix, Brazil, in n. 45; 'The Church in Bolivia', in n. 74; pastoral letter of the Mexican bishops in n. 74; 'Eu ouvi os clamores de meu povo', by the bishops and religious superiors of North-East Brazil, in n. 66.

7. 'Eu ouvi . . .', *loc. cit.*, p. 608.

8. Document on justice in the world, in *ibid.*, p. 426.

9. 'Eu ouvi . . .', pp. 627–8.

10. D. Helder Camara, 'As multinacionais: esfinge de nosso tempo', in SEDOC 65 (1973), p. 472.

11. 'Marginalizacão de um povo . . .', in SEDOC 73 (1974), pp. 1010–19.

12. 'Desenvolvimiento e mudanças estructurais', in SEDOC 25 (1970), p. 1259.

13. *Medellín*, Introduction, 4, p. 36.

14. *Medellín, Peace*, 16, p. 55.

15. Homily by D. Marcos McGrath, archbishop of Panama, in SEDOC 56 (1973), p. 884; Cf. also: bishops of Nicaragua in SEDOC 65; letter by the bishop of Corocoro, Bolivia, in n. 45; *Medellín, Peace*, 14–16, pp. 53–5; bishops of Argentina in n. 57; of Nicaragua in n. 54; of Colombia in n. 39.

16. Document on justice in the world, in n. 66, pp. 427–32. Cf. also: Manifesto of the Bishops of the Third World, in SEDOC 6–7, *Cristianismo y revolución* (1968); *Medellín, Justice*, 3, p. 42; Card. J. Landázuri, Address to the University of Notre Dame, quoted in G. Gutiérrez, *A Theology of Liberation* (London, 1974, New York, 1973), p. 126; Conclusions of the Latin-American pastoral Conference, in SEDOC 41; bishops of Nicaragua on 'the Christian and politics', in n. 65; Conclusions of the 36th assembly of Peruvian bishops, in n. 11.

17. On justice in the world, n. 66.

18. Conclusions . . . in n. 11.

19. 'Marginalizacão . . .', in n. 73.

20. Bishops of the Third World, in nn. 6–7.

21. G. Gutierrez, *op. cit.*, pp. 133–38.

22. Mexican bishops, in n. 90; *Medellín, Peace*, 18, pp. 56–58.

23. 'Marginalizacão . . .'

24. *Medellín, Justice*, 13, p. 46; cf. also: Chilean bishops in n. 74.

25. *On justice in the world*, n. 66.

26. Chilean bishops in n. 49.

27. Argentinian bishops in n. 57.

28. Chilean bishops in n. 90.

29. On criticism of anti-communism: Mexican bishops in n. 90; Chilean bishops in n. 74; *idem.* in n. 49; declaration of the Social Action dept. of CELAM in n. 59; 'Desenvolvimiento . . .', in n. 25.

30. *Medellín, Peace*, 15, 19, pp. 55–6.

31. *ibid.*, p. 55.

32. Conclusions . . . in n. 11; Mexican bishops in n. 90; bishops of Nicaragua in n. 65.

33. D. Marcos McGrath in n. 56.

34. D. Sergio Méndez Arceo, 'Proyección y transformación de la iglesia en Latinoamerica', quoted in Gutiérrez, *op. cit.*, p. 127.

35. Bishops of the Third World in nn. 6–7.

36. 'Eu ouvi . . .' in n. 66.

37. D. S. Méndez Arceo in n. 54, and interviewed in n. 49.

38. Justice in the world, in n. 66.

39. *Ibid.*

40. D. S. Méndez Arceo in n. 54.

41. 'Eu ouvi . . .' in n. 66; cf. also, Gutiérrez, *op. cit.*, pp. 133–38; D. Alberto Devoto, bishop of Goya, Argentina. 'Pronunciamento' of January 1973, printed in *Cristianismo y Sociedad* 1–2 (1973).

Other sources: Bishops' Commission for social action, *Signos de Renovación*, a collection of post-Conciliar documents of the Church in Latin America (Lima, 1969); *Signos de liberación: Testimonios de la Iglesia en América Latina 1969–73* (Lima, 1973); *Iglesia Latinoamericana: protesta o profecía?* (Avellaneda, 1969); *La Iglesia Latinoamericana y el Socialismo*, hierarchical and church group documents, ed. INDAL (Information documentaire d'Amérique Latine) (Belgium), Dossier no. 8, 1973.

42. D. S. Méndez Arceo in SEDOC 54.

43. Bishops of Nicaragua in SEDOC 65.

Ignacio Ellacuría

The Function of Economic Theories in Theological-Theoretical Discussion on the Relationship between Christianity and Socialism

THE subject can be divided into two basic sections: (1) theological-theoretical discussion on the relationship between Christianity and socialism; (2) the function of economic theory in this discussion. I propose moreover to approach the problem from a Third World point of view and from a particular economic theory, the theory of dependence. So without further semantic elucidations on the theme and its divisions let us move straight into the discussion.

From the point of view of Latin American theology[1] the need for theological-theoretical discussion between Christianity and socialism is clear enough. A confrontation between the two is made inevitable by two basic principles—besides the historical urgency: the first is the necessary relationship between the history of salvation and salvation in (and of) history; the second, which follows from the first, is the need Christianity has of historical mediations—both theoretical and practical—if it is to develop its understanding of faith and its realization of salvation.

The connection between the history of salvation and the salvation of history belongs to the essence of God's communication with man as seen by scripture from Genisis to the Apocalypse. One of its versions is the alliance in any of its various formulations, for example: "You have recognized the Lord this day as your God . . . The Lord has recognized you this day as his special possession, as he promised you . . . he will raise you high above all nations . . . and (you will) be a people holy to the Lord your God "(Dt. 26:17–19). "There will never be any poor among you if only you obey the Lord your God by carefully keeping these commandments which I lay upon you this day . . ." (Dt. 15:4–5).

In particular the, 'I will be your God and you will be my people', marks the deep connection between the saving God and history and between saved history and God.

For salvation to be historical it has to relate to human history, has to become historicized.[2] One of the recent breakthroughs in theology has been its new examination of the mystery of God in terms of the history of salvation, although it has still not drawn all the consequences from this breakthrough after either in terms of history or in terms of salvation. The historicity of salvation requires an authentic annunciation of the whole of salvation; it requires an actual presence and a historical realization. The salvation announced to take shape in history requires an opening to the future, requires it to be preparing for the manifestation of the glory of God, the second coming of the Lord of history in the transformations wrought in history. Historical salvation, the fact that the Kingdom of God is progressively being brought about in history, is the constitutive—and not only manifestative—sign of the deifying and saving presence of God incarnate in humanity. It is only a sign, because it is not God himself, but it is a constituted sign, because it is the historic body of salvation, its proper context of realization and verification.

If we are looking for the bringing out of the Kingdom of God in history there is clearly a need for historic mediations. The incarnate God and deified Flesh suppose the unity of two extremes in one mediation which must have something of the two extremes, not necessarily in the order of imitation or likeness, but rather in the order of a dynamic becoming and bringing about of a presence.

If one takes the question in its whole breadth, it is obvious that history is the supreme mediation of the saving encounter of man with God: we know what God is and what God requires of men by the works of God seen in history, and man's personal access to God is brought about by man's work in history. History too shows us the mediator *par excellence*, Jesus of Nazareth, whose mediating function has two aspects of particular concern: the incarnatory aspect by which God became present among men in the visibility of his historical figure and his historical actions, and the redeeming activity by which He became historically the reconciliation of sinful man with God. Together with these two aspects and providing them with their particular historical configuration stands the mediating aspect of following, by which the *life* of Jesus becomes the *truth* of God for man and of man for God, and the *way* by which man's access to God and God's access to man is made possible.

It is this very incarnatory and mediating activity that makes us look for those particular mediations that seek to give flesh to the Kingdom of God in history, but in such a way that the mediation does not subordinate the Kingdom to itself or go on to mediate something else. The Kingdom of God implies the effective presence of God in the world of men, but this in turn means that not any action or course of action can be considered as an *adequate* realization of the Kingdom of God. On the other hand, mediation cannot be confused with either of the two extremes; this means that it cannot be judged either by the criteria proper to the transcendent extreme, nor those proper to a purely human project.

Historical mediation has to be such that in seeking the salvation of history and the full humanization of man and society it does not close man in on himself but leads him to a meeting with Him who is greater than man and than history. A historical salvation that does not bring human solidarity with it is not historical salvation and neither is it history of salvation; a historical salvation that does not open man toward what transcends man in himself cannot be a sign of God, cannot be a history of salvation, and neither can it be the full salvation of history.

The relationship between Christianity and socialism should be set in this theological-theoretical context. It is clear that socialism very definitely seeks human solidarity through justice. It is clear that it seeks historical salvation not only of one or another man or of the sum total of all individuals, but of the people taken all together—even if through a redeeming class. It is also clear that Christianity must seek historical salvation as the sign of the history of salvation. There is therefore no reason for either politicans or churchmen to be surprised that the two movements have a necessary connection despite one seeing the problem more from the point of view of history and the other more from the point of view of God. It is not just a matter, as used to be said, of the Christian being also a citizen; on a deeper level it is a matter of history itself being the context of revelation—or of the absence of revelation—of God and of the fulfillment of man—or of his alienation. Christianity needs to fulfil itself in history, not only as a gift of God but also as the transformation of man; socialism needs to fulfil itself in history as the transformation of man and as a break with a world of injustice, the only way to arrive at a world of brotherhood. This is the theological-theoretical root of the connection between the two.

If one looks at the problem from another standpoint, it can be seen as the question of faith and justice or the struggle for faith and of the struggle for justice. There can be no Christianity without a struggle for justice. Political movements whose basic principle is the quest for and implementation of justice face Christianity with the unavoidable question of whether it is not rather they, above all in particular historical circumstances, who provide the necessary mediation for faith to bring about justice and for justice to open itself to faith.

THE THEORY OF DEPENDENCE

The foregoing paragraphs offer an initial response to the question of the function of economic theories in a theological discussion. Whether one likes it or not, it is a fact that economic structures play a basic part in structuring history on all its levels. Furthermore, although one does not need to accept that social consciousness is a pure reflection of the economic structure, it is impossible to deny the importance of the latter in forming the former and therefore in forming something that has much to do with the history of salvation and with the manner in which it is presented and expressed. Today it is less possible than ever before to see historical salvation apart from a restructuring of the economic system understood as a whole: it is impossible to see the achievement of justice without a basic revolution in the social and economic order, or a true fulfilment of man without bringing an adequate economic structure into operation.

The theory of dependence as opposed to any theory of development sees this with a clarity matching that of the southern skies under which it took shape.[3] Taken as a whole the theory of development gives rise to an interpretation which keeps the underdeveloped countries more and more in bondage—a development of underdevelopment—whereas the theory of dependence arose in Latin America as an effort to unmask imperialism from the countries that are victims of it. For this reason it is more closely related to Marxism and presents Christianity—taken as the means of bringing about historical salvation—with an important challenge.

The idea of development is seen in Latin America as an ideology that conceals the reality of the process. Starting with recognition of the fact of underdevelopment it goes on to suppose that its solution consists in imitating the model of the developed countries without an adequate analysis of the historical roots of underdevelopment or their structural context. This ideology supposes that there is only a difference of degree between underdevelopment and development, so that one can go from one to the other without a break; all that is needed is evolution and not revolution. This interpretation gives rise to an ideologized theology which starts with the fact of creation but then leaves aside the existence of sin and the break represented by the death of Jesus; consequently it rejects all praxis that might suppose any form of struggle or revolution. The fact that this has been the dominant theological ideology of Latin America, first through Latin America's condition as a colonized continent and the identification of ecclesiastical interests with the ruling class, and secondly through the supposed modernization implied in its involvement in the process of development, is the best proof of the deep inter-relation between economic structure and religious ideology.

There is now a socio-economic theory opposed to this developmenttist position, which sees the present situation of underdevelopment as the result of a historical process crystalized in different national structures: some are underdeveloped *because* others are developed. The domination-dependence syndrome is the result of an unjust historical process and not of natural circumstances. This interpretation gives rise to the theology of liberation.[1] This accepts the creation but immediately goes on to insist on the sin of the world, which arises from history rather than from nature to oppress both history and nature; it takes the journey of the people of God from a historical situation of oppression to an also historical situation of salvation as its model of salvation; it therefore sees the need for a historical struggle and the imposition of a new society, one that breaks with all structures of domination; it sees the example of this in the historical life of Jesus and his confrontation even unto death with the powers of the world; it sees finally a Church whose institutional form no longer follows models of oppression but is changed into a source of prophecy and witness in its accompaniment of the oppressed people of God. Seen in broad terms, the theory of dependence not only offers theology new possibilities but shows the way to reconcile Christian praxis with secular political praxis in a unity without confusion. Let us examine a few points that show this in practice.

The first is the existence of the *Third World* as a reality both socioeconomic and theological. The Third World is not only the historical setting for the fact of domination: it is also the theological setting for the fact of sin. Even if this simile cannot be taken to the extreme, one can say that it bears the sins of the world without having committed them. The Third World is the historical truth of all imperialism and in this sense it is the prophet who by his presence alone shows what sin is and what its historical structure is. The Third World has many of the characteristics of the suffering servant of Yahweh and so bears the promise of carrying the hidden Christ in its midst, of being the historical body of Christ. The Third World therefore does not mean the entire society of Asia, Africa and Latin America but its suppressed and dominated majorities. It has thus a redemptive and saving mission, a mission which it has to accomplish in history as did the oppressed people of Israel, and it has to carry out this mission through historical actions, which will not lessen the deep theological significance of its struggle for justice.

The dominant nations project their *structures of production* and *structures of consumption* on this Third World through the production of surplus and the market structure which enables them to take advantage of surplus production. It is this putting of surplus on to the market that closes the process and brings about what is called the consumer society. With regard to production, it calls capital factors of human achievement into operation, and with regard to consumption, it duplicates the conditions of domination. The riches-poverty duality with its basic structure of a relationship of oppression between one and the other both at the moment of production and at the moment of consumption leads to the destruction of those relationships without which man can neither be at peace with himself nor find unity with his fellow man nor find a way of access to God. The brute fact is that the consumer society and its root, the production society, are consuming both man and the world, are destroying both. The theory of dependence makes this clear and has a natural affinity to what should be the Christian approach.

This means that the basic historical task of those countries that are suffering from economic, political, cultural and religious oppression can only have one name: *liberation*. The political success of this term stems from the fact that it goes to the root of both the objective conditions and the dawning subjective conditions of the oppressed peoples and classes; its theological success derives on the one hand from being one of the most all-embracing concepts in the history of salvation, and on the other from its response to the need to connect the history of salvation with the saving of history. The Christian maintains that there can be no overall liberation without the operative strength of the spirit of Christ in history, but he also maintains that there can be no specifically Christian liberation without this becoming fact in history, and this requires historical mediations. Only a re-interpretation of the fact of the Third World and of the production-consumer society from the standpoint of an adequate economic theory can lead to an adequate theory of liberation and an effective praxis of liberation: at the same time only by applying faith and theological reflection to the theoretical and practical processes of liberation will it be possible to make faith meaningful and to make it operative in history.

There is no space here even to allude to the works in which the theory of dependence and theology of liberation have begun their task of unifying historical salvation and the history of salvation. What is happening in fact is that the existence of the theory of dependence is forcing theology to undertake two fundamental tasks: the first is a critical re-thinking of all the theological formulations and Christian practices which are unconsciously dependent on economic structures whose intimate result can only be one of domination; the second is a positive new approach to how Christian faith and praxis should be conceived at a historical moment and in a structural situation such as the one described by the theory of dependence and, beyond the theory of dependence, by brute reality itself. It is no exaggeration to state that this double re-reading, both negative and positive, critical and constructive, will lead to a drastic reformulation of our idea of God, our idea of Jesus Christ, our idea of salvation, our idea of the Church, our idea of pastoral practice. So there is a whole new theological task to be tackled, in which the unmasking process achieved by the theory of dependence and the new problems it poses represent a theoretical and practical challenge of the first order. In a sense it is taking theology back to its origins and providing it with a source of inspiration similar to those of the richest moments of revelation. The theology that emerges will no longer be one that defends domination nor even the institutional interests of the Church but one living from the very sources of faith.

Economic theories in themselves pose grave problems for the whole theological undertaking and this is particularly true of the theory of dependence which describes in socio-economic terms a reality that the history of salvation itself has described a thousand times in historico-theological terms.

It must be said of both the theory of dependence and of the theology of liberation that, at present, they are not adequate as models for action; this applies to the theology of liberation because this is not its prime task, and to the theory of dependence because it lies more in the field of diagnosis and denunciation than of solutions.

This is where socialism—and this does not mean bourgeois socialism or utopian socialism—comes into play as an effective praxis which paradoxically places human values above economic values. The theory of dependence is a subsidiary of Marxist theory although it represents a new opening of this to a new historical situation. Its critique of a mechanical application of orthodox Marxist ideology is a good point on which to hang theological discussion on the relationship between Christianity and socialism.

This relationship is certainly not devoid of dangers but perhaps there are greater dangers in leaving it aside or denying its value. Identifying the history of salvation too far with a particular historical project can lead to a loss of its meaning in both theory and practice, to forgetting what the eschatological reserve requires. But neither can one pass over the meaning that historical events such as those represented by Nebuchadnezzar or Cyrus or the part played by the Roman Empire in the destruction of the temple in Jerusalem mean for the history of salvation. None of them can be held to represent either belief or justice but they nevertheless represented a step towards integration in the history of salvation.

Translated by Paul Burns

Notes

1. Cf. Various, *Liberación y Cautiverio* (Mexico, 1975); Various, *Método teológico y cristología latinoamericana* (San Salvador, 1975); I. Ellacuría, 'Tesis sobre posibilidad, necesidad y sentido de una teología latinoamericana', in Various, *Teología y mundo contemporáneo* (Madrid, 1975), pp. 325–50.

2. I. Ellacuríta, *Freedom Made Flesh* (New York, 1976).

3. I understand the theory of development as opposed to the theory of dependence, and *only* as this. Cf. Various, *América Latina: dependencia y subdesarollo* (San José, 1975).

4. In view of the short space allowed for this article and the breadth of the subject, I am unable to go into the historical and theoretical complexity of the assertions made in the text.

Contributors

VICTOR MANUEL ARBELOA Y MURU was born in Maneru, Navarra, Spain, and is now engaged in research into the Church and workers' movements. He is professor of political and ecclesiastical history at the Pastoral Institute, Madrid, and the Theological Studies Centre, Pamplona, Spain.

GREGORY BAUM was born in Berlin and has been in Canada since 1940. He is professor of theology and sociology at St Michael's College, Toronto University. Among his many major works is *Religion and Alienation* (1975).

FERNANDO CASTILLO was born in Santiago de Chile. His doctoral thesis (Münster) was on the problem of praxis in the theology of liberation. He is now resident in England.

IGNACIO ELLACURIA studied under Karl Rahner. He is director of the Theological Studies Centre of El Salvador. His most recent publication is *Freedom Made Flesh* (New York, 1976).

IRING FETSCHER was born in Marbach am Neckar, Germany. He is one of the world's leading experts on socialism and Marxism, and he has published several works on Hegel, Marx, Rousseau and Marxism. In 1976 he was visiting fellow at the Research School of Social Sciences of the Australian National University.

MATIAS GARCIA-GOMEZ, S. J., is professor of pastoral and moral theology at Granada University, Spain. He was rector of the Faculty of Theology there from 1968 to 1974.

JOSE MARIA GONZALEZ-ESTEFANI Y ROBLES was born in Torredonjimeno, Spain. He is professor in the Faculty of Sociology of the Pontifical University at Salamanca. His most recent publication is on messianism and secularization in contemporary social movements.

HANS-HERMANN HÜCKING was born in Göttingen, Germany. Since 1971 he has lectured on philosophy at the Westphalia College in Dortmund.

IVO DO AMARAL LESBAUPIN was born in Rio de Janeiro, Brazil. He is now a post-graduate student of theology. One of his major works is a study of Christian life in the Roman Empire.

NGUYEN QUOC-HUNG is a leading journalist specializing in southeast Asia and working in Paris. He is a member of the permanent bureau of the Fraternité Vietnam organization and has recently completed a fact-finding mission of six months' duration in Asia.

GIUSEPPE RUGGIERI was born in Pozzallo, Italy. He is professor of fundamental theology at the Gregorian University, Rome. He teaches fundamental theology at the Theological Studies Centre of S. Paulo di Catania. Among his publications are studies of political theology and faith and theology.

HANSJAKOB STEHLE has been a permanent correspondent for *Die Zeit* of Hamburg and a German radio correspondent in Rome. Among his publications is a study of society and politics in Poland and a major study of the eastern European politics of the Vatican, soon to be published in English by Ohio University Press.

MICHAEL TRABER was born in Zürich, Switzerland. From 1961 to 1970 he directed the Mambo Press communications centre in Gwelo, Rhodesia. He was at the Africa Literature Centre in Kitwe, Zambia, in 1973. He has published works on racism and revolutionary Africa.

PHILIPPE WARNIER is a member of a French grass-roots community, and is active at an organizational level in the base communities movement in France. He has written and published books on the subject and on Christian revolution.

RUDOLF WEILER was born in Vienna. Since 1970 he has been director of the Institute for Peace Research at the University of Vienna where he has been professor of ethics and social sciences since 1966. He has published on economic co-operation, peace and decision processes.

KUNO FÜSSEL was born in Trier, Germany. He is research assistant in Catholic theology at the University of Münster and has published in the fields of political theology, futurology and scientific theory.